Preparing for Liturgy

A Theology and Spirituality

Preparing for Liturgy

A Theology and Spirituality

AUSTIN FLEMING

The Pastoral Press
Washington, D.C.

ISBN: 0-912405-16-3

The Pastoral Press
225 Sheridan Street, NW
Washington, D.C. 20011
(202) 723-5800

The Pastoral Press is the publications division of the National Association of Pastoral Musicians, a membership organization of musicians and clergy dedicated to fostering the art of musical liturgy.

Printed in the United States of America

Table of Contents

Foreword 1

1   Back to Basics. 3
    Whom Do We Worship?
    Why Do We Worship?
    How Do We Worship?
    Putting Theory Into Practice

2   Let's Stop Planning Liturgies! 31
    Liturgy Cannot Be Planned...
    Liturgy Must Always Be Prepared...
    A Ministry, and Therefore An Art...
    Patron Saints For Those
              Who Prepare for Worship

3   Speaking of Liturgy. . . . . : 43
    Traditional and Contemporary
    The Popular Sense of "Traditional"
              and "Contemporary"
    Formal and Informal
    Styles of Worship
    Creative Liturgy

4   Living the Tradition: A Contemporary Task. 71
    Building Cathedrals
    New "Traditions"

5   Spirituality and Liturgical Ministry 81
    Spiritual Intimacy
    A Spirituality For Liturgical Ministers
    Ministries and Spiritualities
    Reflections for Liturgical Ministers
    One Bread, One Cup, One Ministry

Blessing and Dismissal 109
    Blessing
    Dismissal

Acknowledgments

This is a small book but its roots are many; failure to acknowledge them would be an injustice.

My worship experience in three very different communities provides much of the background for the pages that follow. I am indebted to: the people of St. Ann Parish in Wollaston, Massachusetts, who prayed patiently with me and for me in the early days of my presbyterate; the staff and students of Morrissey Manor at the University of Notre Dame, who provided sanctuary for my heart and prayer for four wonderful years; the people of St. Ann Parish and Student Center in Boston, who have reverenced and reverently challenged my share in the Lord's ministry for them.

The faculty for the Master's Program in Liturgical Studies at the University of Notre Dame, especially Robert Taft, S.J., and Mark Searle, have influenced these pages beyond what any footnote might credit.

Two friends have offered constant support and affection: Rev. Frank Fairbairn, fellow minister and mentor in truly pastoral theology; Jane Pitz, C.S.J., who has helped me to see with an artist's eye and to touch gently the life which the liturgy celebrates.

Finally, my thanks to Mary Ellen Cohn and Dan Connors of the Pastoral Press whose patience has been a blessing in this venture.

Foreword

This book is about worship: in particular it is about the liturgy of the Roman Catholic communion. The principles at work in this text are those that undergird the whole of liturgical prayer: the celebration of the sacraments and their attendant rites, and of the Liturgy of the Hours. At the risk of furthering the misconception that the liturgy is exhausted in the celebration of eucharist, these pages will refer often to the liturgy of Sunday mass. The risk is run in favor of finding a ground for discussion common to most readers.

This book is written for believers, especially those whose belief has enkindled in them a deep love for the ritual of God's people at prayer. The author is one among this impassioned group and recognizes that such a combination of reader and writer is a combustible one. In some ways I will be perceived as the visitor on Christmas Eve who critiques the way your family has decorated its Christmas tree. In this analogy even Mr. Scrooge would fare better than such a meddling stranger! Rest assured: I would most likely tell you that your family's tree was the best in town, no matter how the misshapen fir might be festooned. After all, it is *your tree* and my family has its own. But the liturgy is yours only because it is the *Lord's* and because it is the Lord's, it is mine, too.

The Christmas tree in your living room will be pitched out after New Year's or (in ecologically motivated families) planted in your back yard to serve another purpose. But the liturgy is no throw-away and its purpose is one and constant in the life of the church. Liturgy is not the property of each or any one community: it is the prayer of the whole church precisely because it it the *Lord's* prayer in which all of us have a share. This book is offered as a context in which a conversation about our share in Christ's prayer might begin.

It is not my intent to pass judgment on the prayer of any community. Nevertheless, I hope to articulate some principles in language strong enough to prompt a good, hard look at how the prayer of the larger church is translated into the ritual language of each community's faith experience. In the long run, the criteria for judgment are not based in any particular school of liturgical thought; the criteria devolve from our fidelity to the Lord's word, our share in the dying and rising of Jesus, and our affection for what is handed down to us in that traditioned community that is the body of Christ.

Chapter 1

Back to Basics

A five-year-old walked into the living room just as her parents' neighborhood bible study group completed its discussion of the images of Christ in the gospels of Matthew, Mark, and Luke. The child asked what the grownups had been talking about and was told, "We talked about God, sweetheart." The little one rejoined, "Who is God?" The silent tension in the room would only have been heightened if the next question had been, "Where do babies come from?"

The simplest questions are often the most provocative and especially so when posed by children. Perhaps this is why the *youngest* member of the Jewish family is prompted to ask, at the Passover table, "Why is this night different from all other nights?" There is a depth and disarming honesty in a child's artlessness that cannot be dismissed as merely simplistic and that will not be satisfied by complexities that beg the question.

The Seder meal certainly provides a better environment for a child's query than did the bible study in the story above. The difference in the two settings is telling: in the latter we find adults who had *finished* asking the questions; in the former we meet those who are waiting for the question to be asked again and again—from the guileless lips of a child. There is an uncanny wisdom among the elders who wait each year to hear and to learn from the child's question.

Following the lead of our Semitic brothers and sisters, you are invited to recapture that bold innocence which is so much the gifted beauty of the children around us. The questions we

3

are about to ask of worship are simple and provocative. These are questions we have asked before; questions we have "answered" before. Our purpose in posing them again is twofold: to see if we have become too easily content with half or false answers; and to delve once more into the mystery of those questions the asking of which is ever the task of believers.

Remember when?

The month was September; the year (1925, 1935, 1945, 1955) made little difference; the questions were the same:

Who made the world?

Who is God?

Why did God make you?

You were in your second week of religious education classes at St. Anyone Parish. Most of the teachers were women, dressed in religious garb, who all responded to the same name, "Sister." Your assignment had been to memorize the answers to the first page of questions in the *Baltimore Catechism;* your hope and goal were to answer perfectly so that a gold star might be affixed to that same page.

Those of us whose first sharing in the eucharist predates the opening of the Second Vatican Council have such scenes etched in our religious memories. The pedagogy, for weal or for woe, has changed, but the import, value and content of the questions remain constant. Questions of this kind are the ones we put to worship:

Whom do we worship?

Why do we worship?

How do we worship?

Remember: these are questions whose depth and honesty cannot be dismissed as merely simplistic and which will not be satisfied by complexities that beg the question. We make our inquiry with a child's naiveté, hoping to disabuse ourselves of "adult" presumptions and preconceptions.

4

Whom Do We Worship?

We worship God. Paraphrasing *Webster's*, the christian expands this simple answer with a profession of faith: we show religious devotion and reverence in a service or rite; in prayer, we adore and venerate the Deity as Creator, Redeemer, and Sustainer. Worship, then, is directed towards and offered to — is *for* — God.

The preposition *for*, in the last sentence, is a significant one and deserving of further reflection. If worship is *for* God, where do we, the worshipers, fit in this scheme of holy things? Is it not true that in some sense worship is *for* us who offer it? An analogy with wakes and funerals may be helpful here. Is the *Rite of Christian Burial* (in all its vigil, processional and eucharistic expressions) *for* the deceased or *for* the surviving community of believers? The christian answers that such ritual is for both the faithful one departed and the faithful ones remaining. "We would have you be clear about those who sleep in death, brothers; otherwise you might yield to grief, like those who have no hope. For if we believe that Jesus died and rose, God will bring forth with him from the dead those also who have fallen asleep believing in him" (I Thes. 4:13-14).

The community gathers to pray for the *bringing forth* of the deceased and in doing so we pray *for* the dead. In praying for the dead we console one another with this message: both in life and in death we are the Lord's (I Thes. 4:18, Rom. 14:8); thus, our prayer is for *us*, too.

The weakness in this analogy is that it sets aside, for the moment, our initial question, "Whom do we worship?"; its strength lies in demonstrating that prayer can benefit both the *prayers* and the ones *for whom* we pray. If *worship* is for *God*, can it also be for *those who worship?* The distinction made here is not one of mere semantic quibbling. When our ancestors in the faith failed to appreciate the difference, they fashioned a golden idol for themselves. The distinction is the difference between worship and the potential for idolatry.

The temptation to miss the difference is still with us and is one into which we pray not to be led.

Before the Council...

For hundreds of years (until the reforms of 1963),[1] even the casual bystander at mass in a Roman Catholic church would have concluded that worship was for God. Our memory of those days is sometimes tainted by a nostalgic reverie and we would do well to keep this in mind. Nevertheless, the gathering of hundreds of people on a Sunday morning, kneeling in silent prayer until a ringing bell announced the entrance of priest and servers in the sanctuary did create an ambience which directed most attention away from ourselves and towards that central figure behind the altar rail — *alter Christus* — whose ministry it was to offer the holy sacrifice. This he did not so much with "his back to the people," but oriented towards the reserved sacrament in the tabernacle, from which store the faithful would receive the eucharist. Those who followed an English translation in hand missals would be aware of these significant words in the Roman canon: "Almighty God, we pray that your angel may take this sacrifice to your altar in heaven" (Eucharistic Prayer I). These words the priest prayed quietly, with head bowed and hands joined. The incense, ceremony, and haunting chants of what we called "high mass" served to heighten our appreciation that what we were doing, we were doing for God.

...And after the Council

Such worship is no longer normative in the Roman rite. We have moved towards a restoration of our worship such that texts and rites "more clearly (express) the holy things they signify; (that) the christian people, so far as possible, should be enabled to understand them with ease and to take part in them fully, actively, and as befits a community."[2]

[1]Beginning with the promulgation of the *Constitution on the Sacred Liturgy (CSL)*, on 4 December 1963.
[2]*Constitution on the Sacred Liturgy*, no. 21, *Documents of Vatican II*, ed. Walter M. Abbott, (New York, N.Y.: America Press, 1966).

There is a tendency for us to look down our noses at the pre-Conciliar liturgy and to pat ourselves on the back for what we have done to reform it. (Our reverie is not confined to nostalgia!) We easily forget that these older prayer forms were the faith expressions of our forebears whose fidelity to Christ's command, "Do this in memory of me," preserved for our own generation the meal and message of the new covenant. (It was the Israelites' impatience with the *way* Moses was doing things that led to the gathering and melting down of jewelry.) Worship, be it pre- or post-Conciliar, always runs the risk of becoming an idol, of becoming an end unto itself.

Whom do we worship? Is worship for *God* or for *us* — or for *both?* The response is a sobering reflection away from us.

No more prayer!

Suppose that for some strange reason christians around the world stopped praying tomorrow: no more private prayer, no more public prayer; no more hymn singing; no more sacraments; no more prayer or bible study groups; no more preaching; no more worship.

Would God be any the less for all this?

Would God begin to pine for the days when heaven was stormed with prayer and thanksgiving?

Would God feel empty or lonely?

The answer to all three questions is a disquieting "No." There is nothing that we are, nothing that we have, and nothing we can do for which God has a *need*. Nothing.

We need to remember that God does not need *us*. In fact, God has never needed us. God did not need the first man and woman in Eden — but God created them anyway. For that matter, God had no need of the rest of creation either, but chose to create the world purely out of love. The God whom we worship needs neither us nor our prayer.

Uncle Harry's Christmas gift

This is good news! Suppose that God did need something

from us: what would we offer? All that we have and all that we are is already God's gift to us. The best we can do is to rewrap God's gifts to us and present them to their, and our, Creator as though they were from us. It's one thing to rewrap the gift your Uncle Harry sent you for Christmas last year and to give it to your neighbor this year. It's another thing altogether to send the rewrapped present back to Uncle Harry for his birthday! Thank God: what Uncle Harry would find insulting, the Creator finds delightful.

> . . . all powerful and ever-living God,
> we do well always and everywhere to give you thanks.
> You have no need of our praise,
> yet our desire to thank you is itself your gift.
> Our prayer of thanksgiving adds nothing to your greatness,
> but makes us grow in your grace . . . (Preface for weekdays IV).

"Our desire to thank you is itself your gift" to us. Isn't that strange? God, who has no need of our prayer, puts within us the desire to worship. Should we conclude, then, that worship is for our own sakes; that worship is for *us*? Our response here cannot be without some subtlety and ambiguity: all of our worship is given to God who has no need of it but who does accept it; we offer that worship precisely *because* it is "our duty and our salvation" to do so.

We have stumbled upon the second of our "back to basics" questions: "Why do we worship?" Because the three questions are intimately connected, we will need to look at the "why" of worship before drawing out the implications of the sobering assertion that God has no need of our prayer.

Why Do We Worship?

Consider the difference between these two statements:

1) *It is April 14 and I need to pay my taxes.*
2) *It is April 14 and I have a need to make a contribution to the Internal Revenue Service; I will pay my taxes.*

The first statement is made out of a sense of duty, obligation, and imposed expectations; the second is made out of a

8

desire, "a felt need," which may or may not be linked with external pressures. In order to understand "why" we worship (that it is our duty and our salvation), we first had to acknowledge that God has no need of our worship. To further understand the "why" of worship we must investigate which kind of "need" prompts the worship we offer.

Our need to worship may stem from that internal desire (God's gift to us), or from external obligation (as announced by scripture, church ordinance, family or peer pressure). Do some folks have one kind of need and other folks the other? No, we all have both. Regardless of our openness to it, God is always planting within us the desire to pray and offer worship. In addition, there is always set before the believing community the announced obligation to worship, which is ours by baptism and membership in the church. (In this way, one sees that external obligation is more support than hindrance in our freedom to respond to God's activity in our lives.) To give God "thanks and praise, always and everywhere" is our duty and our salvation: whether we feel it or not; whether we *feel like* it or not.

Feelings and needs

In our own times, this approach is nothing short of counter-cultural:

Consider the coin of the day:
If it feels good. . .
I know I should have done that, but I just didn't feel like doing it, and what's the sense if your heart isn't in it?
I'll get around to it when I really feel up to it.
I know that's what I said, but when I said it I didn't know how I was going to feel about it now.

We have all heard, or made, these or similar statements; we all have heard touted the value of "going with your gut feelings." This book's purpose is not the debunking of "pop psychology," neither is it to critique the ethic of a cultural psyche. All this notwithstanding, we cannot deny that "feelings" have recently played a significant role in the way many Catholic christians approach worship. In some instances, feelings determine "whether or not I'll go to mass;" and feelings are often the subtle and final arbiter in determining what is "good liturgy" and what is not.

The caution is this: feelings sometimes serve as a subtle way of insuring that I do what *I* like; what is best for *me*; what is easiest for *me*. When it comes to keeping my word or responding to demands that originate from an authority outside of myself, feelings are often a shaky basis for decision and action. In a culture that seems ready to surrender so much authority to feelings, we christians would do well to remember that Christ preached a love that is *law*, not a feeling. (Is it possible that some of those camped at the base of Mt. Sinai *felt* that it was time to fashion an idol?)

Why we worship

Our need to worship rises out of that God-given desire that is the Creator's gift to us and is supported by that community of believers whose structure and faith announce that worship is our duty and our salvation. Our salvation rests in praising and thanking God who has no need of our praise and thanks. This is why we worship: God made us, God loves us (even in our sin), and God saves us. To put it simply: God has done a lot for us and we are in debt to God up to our ears! And the debt is even greater than simply what we owe our saving God for our redemption. Jesus, in the Easter mystery of his dying and rising, *has paid the debt for us.* We owe a debt to God — and — we owe God for letting the debt be written off in the gift of Christ's life for us.

How do we pay back a debt when the one we owe has canceled the debt? We don't — because we can't — but we ought to be mighty thankful and filled with praise for the one we owe. And that's the way it is between God and us: whether we like it or not; whether we *feel* like it or not.

In this relationship there are significant inequalities; not all the parties are equal. We, the children of creation, are equal in that we all owe God a debt of thanks and praise (worship). The inequality is that we are creatures and not the Creator; God made us and not we God. In this relationship we stand

10

poor, with empty hands, before God who fills our emptiness with love, mercy, and life (which, on our own, we do not deserve, cannot earn, nor fully return). God fills our emptiness with that which satisfies the greatest *need* of every human heart.

The naked order of things

We want to know "where we stand" with the people and situations that give shape to our lives. We want to know the boundaries, to test the limits, to find our place. We search out these things in our day to day individual lives and we look for the answers to these questions in the framework of history. The christian names stance, boundaries, and place in terms of relationship with God, recognizing that there is no creature who is self made.

Like our first parents in the garden, we often hide in the foliage, concealing what has been revealed in our attempt to "be like gods." We hear that voice, at the "breezy time of the day," calling, "Where are you? Who told you that you were naked?" Clutching loincloths close to us, we venture out, in our most real nakedness, to stand in the presence of our Creator. What can be our response save a plea for forgiveness and a pledge of praise and thanksgiving when we are pardoned? Why do we worship? Because worship is of the *order* of things, as it will be yet in that reign of God where the original order of creation is fully restored. We worship because worship is the most honest statement we can make about ourselves and the world in which we live. We would do well to consider the alternatives. . . .

Worship is for God

Worship is the most legitimate and consummating of all human activity. It is the process of recognizing the distinctive relationship and the related distinctions of God's relationship with creation. Worship acknowledges debts owed and paid; the acknowledgment expresses itself in praise and thanksgiving. Clearly, worship is God-centered and God-directed. This, however, does not constitute a denial of the fact that we who worship enjoy some benefit from the worship we offer. The mutuality here is the stuff of covenant revealed in scripture.

Worship is clearly for God but it seems just as clear that in some way it is for us, too. How so?

That was a great liturgy!

That was a great liturgy! How often have we made such a statement as we leave a service of worship? How often has it been addressed, as *kudos,* to those whose care is the preparation for and ministry within the liturgy? What does this comment or commendation reveal of our understanding of for whom the liturgy is offered?

That was a great liturgy! Is this another way of saying, "Well! we did a good job today of paying back the debt that can't be paid!"? Perhaps not. In some instances, "great liturgy" may simply indicate that the service did not leave those in attendance bored or disappointed. More often, though, a "great liturgy" is one that touches us, draws us in, speaks to us, and makes us "feel good." Our response to the question, "What makes a great liturgy?" may tell us more than we care to know about ourselves at prayer. Do we come to the worship service for God or for ourselves? Is the quality of worship determined by what it did for us, aesthetically, or by what we did for God? The ideal, of course, is that in doing something for God we know the benefit of what we have done in that we are rendered and surrendered closer to the Lord whom we came to serve.

Entangled in the mystery

Christian worship is born out of the divine humanity of Christ; out of that mystery that we name the Incarnation (enfleshment) of God's Word. We, the community of believers, are forever entangled in this mystery and this is no more poignant and real than when we gather to offer "divine service" — the liturgy. For christians it is never a question of "for God or for us." Such distinctions are simply false in the wake of the gospel. Worship is for God because God is for us;

worship is for us because we are made for God. This is like the chicken-and-egg dilemma, where the answer to "which comes first," is, "God — who made the chickens who lay the eggs." God enjoys a priority in the covenant relationship, a priority that surrendered itself to us in the Paschal mystery. This surrender was for us so that we might know again and forever the saving mercy of the God who made us.

Worship is where human beings experience in a unique way the divine and the truly human. We "need" worship because it is the way for us to experience all that is good and holy. "All that is good and holy," however, does not need to "experience" what is human and imperfect; much less would God need our liturgy for such an experience. Nor does any of this do violence to the axiom that the Sabbath was made for us and not we for the Sabbath.

If worship leaves us untouched, then it has failed. On the other hand, if the liturgy touches us but does not lead us to experience the God we worship, then it has doubly failed for it has left us self-satisfied and self-interested. Self-satisfaction and self-interest are the fruit of the tree that grew in the middle of that ancient garden; this fruit sometimes takes the suspicious shape of a golden calf.

Worship and idolatry

We are tracing here the sometimes fine line between worship of God and idolatry. The distinction is hoary unless we acknowledge the boundary and respect its imperative. This is not to suggest that idols have been crafted and set up for worship in our churches. It is simply to remind us that idolatry is not a thing of the past and to help us see that the worship itself can become an idol. Perhaps our greatest temptation to idolatry is the temptation to "worship" our own worship, to make of it an end in itself. We will suggest later on in these pages that it is our task to preserve the liturgy as a treasure that has been handed down to us, but when such preservation becomes its own reward, the liturgy becomes a *thing*, an object. Because we ourselves are so appropriately enmeshed in the liturgy, we need always to be careful that our worship

13

not become an icon of ourselves. The liturgy is an icon of the Lord's saving mystery in which we surely see our own redeemed reflection, but it must never become a vanity mirror. ("Mirror, mirror, on the wall, whose liturgy is fairest of them all?")

When our worship leads us to God it has about it a fullness, depth, and vitality with which nothing can compare. Worship that leads us back to ourselves, however, is a dead-end street where the worshipers are left to battle out their petty differences in a spirit that is often less than holy. Wisdom lies in knowing the difference and praying accordingly.

Priestly people or pawns

At first glance, what we have said thus far may appear to reduce the role of worshipers to the status of pawns, and in any but the christian scheme of things this would be a valid critique. But we are the *baptized* and this makes all the difference. Our American bishops have put this in beautiful perspective:

> *The most powerful experience of the sacred is found in the celebration and in the persons celebrating, that is, it is found in the action of the assembly;* **the living words, the living gestures, the living sacrifice, the living meal.**[3]

This notion of the primacy of the assembly is not in opposition to what we have argued. We simply need to pay attention to four significant words in the quote from the document: *experience of the sacred.*

The sacred is revealed and experienced in the assembly and its actions. We are the body of Christ: the priestly, royal, and prophetic community that embodies the Risen Lord in its prayer and work. We come to know who we are and what we are called to do by looking upon the face of God imaged in Jesus who is the Lord. The reflection we see is that of the redeemed sinful. The worship community that honestly

[3]*Environment and Art in Catholic Worship (EACW),* no. 29, Bishops' Committee on the Liturgy (Washington, D.C.: United States Catholic Conference, 1978).

acknowledges the fullness of this reflection, that names its own sin and knows its forgiveness in Christ, is the community that meets and celebrates the Lord's mystery in its daily life outside the sanctuary. The community that acknowledges only half of the reflection will be confused by faults in its redeemed self-image or left hopeless in the face of its own sinfulness. The former will be tempted to correct the faults by efforts at "perfecting" its ritual mirror, the liturgy; the latter will be tempted to wallow in self-pity, which is ultimately a form of self-centeredness alien to the liturgy. In each case the sanctuary becomes a false center in the community's life where either worship forms or the worshipers themselves become the focus of attention. The idol here is not a golden calf but rather the *self*, created in its own, not God's, image.

New boundaries

As Aidan Kavanagh, O.S.B., has put it, "When altars become the center of the world, they skid to its edge." The true sanctuary of liturgy is the one that recognizes the world as the sanctuary of creation and redemption. The community that acknowledges its sin understands the sanctuary of liturgy to be a refuge but not an escape for sinners; the community that rejoices in its redemption in Christ is eager to depart the sanctuary of liturgy to proclaim what it has celebrated there. Disciples of the Lord and the gospel know that in Christ the old, and potentially idolatrous, boundaries of God's sanctuary have been radically revised. Sanctuary is no longer the "safe" place we might imagine it to be. It is where we stand most naked before the Creator and so it is where we find ourselves to be most vulnerable.

Whom do we worship? We worship God. Why do we worship? Because God is who God is. (Yahweh means, "I AM WHO AM.") And because we are who we are, worship (thank God!) is for us, too.

How Do We Worship?

We worship God *through*, *with*, and *in* Jesus Christ. In the

15

opening words of each preface in the missal:

Father, it is our duty and our salvation
always and everywhere
to give you thanks
through your beloved Son, Jesus Christ. . .

That Christ is the mediator of the relationship between God and humankind is clear from the central message of the gospel:

The reign of God is at hand!
Repent: turn your hearts to God!
I have come to announce my Father's mercy
and to show you the way home to God
whose prodigal love is for all.
The way home is the way of the cross:
I will walk it for you;
come, follow me!

We do not worship Jesus

Jesus is the announcement and the incarnation of God's reign of mercy in our midst. This mercy is most clearly proclaimed in the dying and rising of Christ, the first fruits of the new creation, in whom the debt of our sin is paid. Ours, now, is the debt of praise and thanksgiving to the Father as we make our way along the path of Jesus.

Jesus is not the object of our worship. Rather, Jesus came to show us *how* to worship. That is why public prayer (with but rare and curious exceptions) is addressed not to Jesus but to the Father whose mercy Jesus reveals. Neither is Jesus simply a tour guide on the way home. Jesus *is* the way home and *is* the channel of God's mercy upon us.

In faith, and in fact, Jesus is so supremely important in this whole business that the prayer of Jesus is the *only* prayer to which God turns an ear. Does God hear my prayer and your prayer? Yes — because our prayer is made *through, with,* and *in* Christ.

Christ Jesus, high priest of the new and eternal covenant,
taking human nature,
introduced into this earthly exile

16

that hymn of praise
which is sung throughout all ages
in the halls of heaven.
Christ joins the entire community to himself,
associating us with his own singing
of this canticle of divine praise.[4]

We pray, if you will, by hopping on the coattails of Jesus whose sacrifice makes him *the* priest (liturgist) of the new Covenant; the one who has offered the perfect sacrifice once, and for all. Jesus is the one who sings eternally before the Creator the acceptable canticle of divine praise. Whether we like it or not, Jesus sings the only song that is heard in heaven; those whose voices would be heard must sing along with Christ.

We worship by joining in that eternal liturgy that Jesus offers. We join in that canticle of praise and thanksgiving offered by the One who sang from the cross, "Father, into your hands I commend my spirit!" We worship through Jesus because Christ is the most honest statement made of humankind. The prayer of Jesus is always heard, as is the prayer of those who worship *through* Christ, *with* Christ, and *in* Christ.

Ritual and our prayer through Christ

If God has no need of our worship, then certainly God has no interest in the seasonal colors of vestments; whether altar servers will grow up to be women or men; or whether the assembly gathers in Sunday-best or Saturday-casual. None of this could possibly make any difference to God. Jesus, who is the revelation of God in our midst, was equally unconcerned with such matters. Most of the rules and guidelines by which we celebrate our public prayer are meaningless in God's eyes; Jesus would be among the first to disregard them, as the gospel accounts indicate. Yet what is meaningless in God's eyes is filled with importance for us—sometimes in healthy ways and sometimes neurotically. Our respect and reverence

[4]*CSL*, no. 83.

17

for the rules and customs associated with our worship are important because they are concerned with *ritual.*

A good friend of mine often responds to the question, "What's new?" with, "Not much; just the ritual." He is implying that life, of late, has been routine and perhaps even boring. Though this is a common enough understanding of the word, it is one of which we need to disabuse ourselves when speaking of worship. (It would be interesting to trace how ritual has come to connote "rote and commonplace.")

For our purposes the following definition of ritual is offered:

> Ritual is the community's *experience* of its belief. Ritual is the community's familiar, commonly accepted, inherited pattern of interaction with others as that community stands before God. Ritual rehearses the story of the community's origins and thus it helps us to know who we are. In ritual activity the divine is revealed in the ordinary and so there is disclosed the value, meaning, and purpose of the world and those who people it. The ritual moment celebrates what is the true order of things and thus preserves us from the threat of chaos.

If we would ponder this definition for a few moments, we would have a deeper understanding of the turmoil, confusion, and anger brought about by the nearly overnight "changes" in our liturgy in the 1960's. The havoc wrought in our worship spaces has yet to cease reverberating. If ritual is our refuge from chaos, then tampering with that ritual can have chaotic repercussions.

Ritual and roots

Ritual tells the story of our roots. It protects us from *amnesia* as it helps us keep alive the memory of how we came to be the people we are. Perhaps the only meaningless or empty ritual is the one that does not tell some people's story.

Ritual activity locates us in the world; it roots us in the ritualizing community and thus provides for us a home. Ritual bonds the individual to the community and precludes aimless wandering; it helps us to know who we are in relation to others and the world. Membership in the ritual community preserves us from the ultimate and radical identity crisis.

18

Religious ritual (all true ritual has about it a religious character) is the patterned way in which the community stands before God. It is the time-tested path and the community's admittance to the holy ground. It is the sanctuary where Creator and creation meet, where the community looks upon the face of God and does not die. It is a particular moment of revelation in which the community experiences the story of its believing. In the telling and the doing (the ritual action(s)) of this story, the community meets its source and sustenance.

Remembering and meeting

It was the day of my grandparents' fiftieth wedding anniversary. The celebration began with a festive eucharist and concluded with a reception and dinner.

At the party I asked my grandfather what had been the best part of the day for him. At first, he was hard put to single out a particular moment but at my insistence he finally allowed that a particular experience was haunting him. He told me that much of the day had been passed in recounting, with friends and family, the "old stories" that had been in the telling for over fifty years: some stories remembered easily, others forgotten but quickly recalled. He said that this had been the heart of the day for him and then offered a gem of grandfatherly wisdom: "You know, when I hear those stories again, it's as if what is past is right here in front of me. It's mysterious."

My grandfather was of French Canadian descent but his comment reflects the wisdom of the Hebrew proverb: *Remembering is a form of meeting*. It is interesting to note that when families gather at Christmas, Thanksgiving Day, funerals, weddings, and reunions, their principal activities are eating and storytelling. Also notable is the fact that most families carry out these two activities according to some familiar, commonly accepted, inherited pattern of interaction. This is why the stranger invited into such gatherings feels literally and figuratively "not at home." No matter how warm and sincere the invitation, the guest knows that he or she is not "related" to the family and the business of its gathering. To

19

meet what is remembered and to take a rightful seat at the feast of that remembrance means that the individual must know well, and have a part in, the story told.

Ritual and experience

If, at the outset, there was some question of what has all of this to do with our prayer *through, with,* and *in Christ,* the last paragraph should hint at some telling implications. Christian ritual is the church's familiar, commonly accepted, inherited pattern of interaction as it stands before God. It is the way in which we tell and do the story of our origins, remembering how we came to be who we are. In christian ritual activity, the divine is revealed in the ordinary (the people; their bread and wine; in water and oil; the spoken word; laying on of hands), and so there is disclosed the value, meaning, and purpose of the world and of those who live in it. Christian ritual names the true order of things and nourishes against the chaos of sin. Our ritual prayer is an *experience* of who and what we believe.

In the assembly's ritual we tell, again and again, the story of our roots as God's people. Never is this telling more articulate than in the celebration of the Paschal Triduum: Holy Thursday, Good Friday, and the Easter Vigil. This one great feast of three days is *the* ritual moment for the family of believers, for in it we rehearse the whole story of our salvation. Is it any wonder that the climax of this three-day feast (the Easter Vigil) should be the premier moment for welcoming, in baptism, new members to have a share in the story and a place at the table of remembrance? Is it not most appropriate that the newly related (baptized) share the communion of the eucharistic table only *after* they have heard the family story in the Vigil's great liturgy of the Word?

Ritual and time

If the Paschal Triduum is the great *annual* christian ritual, then the Sunday assembly for eucharist is the weekly remembrance of the Easter mystery. We gather on the Lord's day not only to tell but also to *do* the story of salvation. The *doing* of the story is our offering of praise and thanksgiving through, with, and in Christ. The form of this *doing* is our prayer and gesture over bread and wine: taking, blessing, breaking and giving. All this we do at the Lord's command: "Do this is *memory* of me." In the eucharist we *meet* the One we *remember*. The Lord is with us! In our ritual we *experience* what we believe: the kingdom is, indeed, *at hand*. Emmanuel is God-with-us.

In all of this we do not "re-enact" the story of salvation. The saving events of the mystery of Jesus happened once, for all, and for all time. We do not somehow restage these events — we remember them. But our meeting the Lord in our remembering is not dependent on our memory or imagination. What we remember is the new Covenant *sealed* in the blood of Christ. This sealing is the guarantee of divine encounter in the remembering of those who are incorporated by baptism into the story of this saving mystery.

The eucharistic feast of remembrance and meeting, however, is not confined to our present encounter with the mystery remembered. The ritual of the eucharist is one of *realized promise:* what we experience is a true glimpse of that great banquet in God's reign where the feasting never ends; where the burdens of the past, the cares of the moment, and anxiousness for the future are subsumed in the unending peace of God's presence. The ritual table of Sunday is promise of home eternal. Thus, the past remembered and the future hoped for are met in the *now*. As much as ritual provides our rootedness, it is equally our strength for the unknown mystery of tomorrow. As much as ritual provides for our rootedness and the identity which flows from those roots, it equally serves as an articulation of what we are yet to become. The fruit of our ritual is the strength for the already and yet-to-be-revealed mystery of God who is our future. Of all this we can be sure because the Lord whom we encounter is God who is, who was, and ever will be.

Given all that we have said of ritual, we should not be surprised that so many laws and customs are protective of our ritual activity. Is it any wonder that tampering with such ritual has the potential of wreaking havoc in the life of the community? We are dealing with those familiar, commonly accepted, inherited patterns of interaction that are the community's path and admittance to the holy ground of encounter with God. The value of the laws and customs that surround our ritual is not inherent in the regulations themselves. Rather, their value lies in the propose they serve: the encounter of God and God's people at a common table for the telling of the story of creation, chaos, and re-creation.

Breaking the rules

There's no denying it: Jesus was the consummate rule-breaker. That's why the Scribes and Pharisees were always on his back. He broke the ritual rules. His greatest ritual crime is reported in the indictment: "This man welcomes sinners and eats with them" (Luke 15:3). Jesus supped (regularly) with the "unclean" — tax collectors, prostitutes, lepers, and outcasts. To add insult to injury, Jesus went about saying, "I assure you that tax collectors and prostitutes are entering the kingdom of God before you" (Matt. 21:31). In other words, the gentiles and the unclean are coming home to God while you who so scrupulously "keep the law" are headed for condemnation.

It was not out of some delinquent or capricious free spirit that Jesus broke the rules, but rather to establish the *new* ritual, the new covenant sacrifice sealed in the blood of the Lamb of God who takes away (cancels the debt of) the sin of the world. This new covenant in Christ's blood is for everyone, and particularly for those whom the old law deemed unclean and sinners.

We who worship through Christ are called to continue in this rule-breaking tradition: to break all the rules that protect us from serving one another; all the rules that divide rather than unite us; all the rules that keep "them," whoever they may be, "in their place." Jesus would break every rule that leads us to believe that "they" are unclean and we are the "saved." Most of all Jesus would condemn whatever leads us to believe that participation in the Sabbath ritual is all that is asked of us.

The new ritual in Christ's blood

"Do this in memory of me. . . ." These are perhaps the least understood of all Christ's words. We are quick to see that we are to continue to celebrate that upper room supper at his bidding; we are slow to recognize that to "do this" in Christ's memory is to break open and pour out ourselves, for others, in fulfillment of the demands of the new Covenant. If we want to know the answer to the question, "How do we worship?" then we should be prepared for a sobering response. Our worship through, with, and in the dying and rising of Jesus is never limited to the sacramentalizing of this mystery at the table of family stories. It means, in *fulfillment* of table prayer, the living out of what we ritualize. St. Paul writes with discomforting clarity on this point:

> *Every time, then, you eat this bread*
> *and drink this cup,*
> *you proclaim the death of the Lord*
> *until he comes!*
> *This means that whoever eats the bread*
> *or drinks the cup of the Lord unworthily*
> *sins against the body and blood of the Lord.*
> *He who eats and drinks*
> *without recognizing the body*
> *eats and drinks a judgment on himself (I Cor. 11:26-29).*

Ritual and judgment

Insofar as we are becoming and living what we eat and drink, we eat the Lord's supper worthily. But when the ritual moment of eucharist becomes an end in itself, not leading us beyond the table to break and pour out our lives in his memory, then we eat and drink a judgment upon ourselves. Having referred to ritual as our path and admittance to the holy ground of encounter with God, we need to remember now that in the Gospel dispensation the ground of divine encounter is the whole of creation. What we do in the defined sanctuary of worship's duty is not an activity *confined* to that sanctuary, but one whose field is the world. At the same

23

time, the story we tell and the ritual gestures we make are *ours*, not simply because they are the church's familiar and inherited patterns of interaction, but because we have *become* that story and have *become* those gestures (which are the Lord's!) in our baptismal dying and rising with Christ. In the Gospel dispensation, the baptized assembly and all its individual members *are* the living rituals of what and who we celebrate: redemption through, with, and in Christ Jesus. Creation is our sanctuary and our baptized lives its ritual.

St. Paul reminds us that those who eat and drink "without recognizing the body," eat and drink a judgment on themselves (I Cor. 11:29). Scripture scholars allow us to understand *body*, here, as referring to the church, the body of Christ. Certainly Paul's holy indignation over what has been reported to him with regard to the Corinthians' gatherings — "One person goes hungry while another gets drunk. . . Would you show contempt for the church of God, and embarrass those who have nothing?" (I Cor. 11:21-22) — justifies this interpretation. In other words: we do not eat the Lord's supper worthily if we do not recognize the Lord's body in our brothers and sisters outside the communion of that table. John's first epistle sums it up: those who say their love is fixed on God, yet hate their neighbors, are liars. If we have no love for our brothers and sisters whom we have seen, we cannot love God whom we have not seen (see I John 4:20).

How do we worship?

We worship through, with, and in Christ the Lord. Christ *is* the way, and there is no other. It was the sacrificial Lamb of the Cross whom the Father received and it is the Lamb's victorious hymn of praise that the Father hears. Christ's sacrifice was once, for all; the sacrifice we offer is one of praise and thanksgiving as a memorial (a remembering) of Jesus' dying and rising. Our sacrifice *is* Christ's, for it is a share in the *sacrificium laudis* (sacrifice of praise), which Christ continually offers before the Father in that sanctuary which has no end.

Having seen that the whole of creation is our sanctuary

and that our baptized lives are its ritual, we can better understand how our offering of thanks and praise is our *duty* and our *salvation*. Our duty does not end and our salvation is not accomplished simply by our share in worship's ritual, but rather by how our prayer together in Christ is an icon of our *life* together in Christ, and for the world. This is why we are able to say that Jesus the rule breaker would most of all reject whatever leads us to believe that participation in the Sabbath and sanctuary ritual is all that is required of us. With Christ, we make the same rejection when we pray that it is our duty and our salvation *always* and *everywhere* to give thanks and praise. Those who ponder and argue the relationship between liturgy and social justice will find in these words the solid link that makes of the two an indivisible unity.

Summing up

Our worship as christians is the gathering of the redeemed sinful on God's holy ground. The joy of this gathering is that we who come empty-handed, offering a prayer which God does not need, are welcomed and heard because our path and admittance to this holy time and place is Christ, our brother and Redeemer. The familiar, commonly accepted, inherited pattern of this sacred encounter and celebration is the dying and rising of Jesus. We live by our share in the One whose life was broken and poured out for our sakes so that we might give of our broken and healed selves for the life of the world. The ritual moment of this encounter anchors us in the embrace of God's loving and merciful arms, where we are most truly at home, so that we might live what we have celebrated, now in the meeting tent of the whole of creation.

We rely, again, on the wisdom of St. Paul:

And now, brothers,
I beg you through the mercy of God
to offer your bodies
as a living sacrifice
holy and acceptable to God, your spiritual worship.
Do not conform yourselves to this age
but be transformed by the renewal of your mind,

so that you may judge what is God's will,
what is good, pleasing and perfect.

(Romans 12:1-2)

and on the revealing beauty of our ritual prayer:

Father, you are holy indeed,
and all creation rightly gives you praise.
All life, all holiness comes from you
through your Son Jesus Christ the Lord,
by the working of the Holy Spirit.
From age to age you gather a people to yourself,
so that from east to west
a perfect offering may be made
to the glory of your name.
And so, Father, we bring you these gifts. . .

(Eucharistic Prayer III)

The children around us would have nodded off to sleep many pages back. They have many years ahead of them to ask these questions, to hear and to tell the story. It is to be hoped, however, that the *child within us* has been refreshed by this exercise, as are the adults and youngsters at the Seder table.

Neither our questions nor our answers are new. We have asked what has been asked for centuries and our response is as old as the questions themselves. In what may appear to be complex, let us pray that we have glimpsed what is provocatively simple.

Putting Theory Into Practice

Our discussion thus far has focused primarily on the liturgy of eucharist celebrated by the community of the baptized. We have referred often to that "canticle of divine praise which Christ Jesus sings throughout all ages in the halls of heaven," which is the sacrifice of praise offered by the church community. The quotation is taken from the *Constitution on the Sacred Liturgy* and it is interesting to note that it is found in the Constitution's chapter on the Liturgy of the Hours. We turn our attention to the Hours by offering a way of putting into practice the theory of this book's first chapter.

*The prayer of the Daily Office (**Liturgy of the Hours**) is part of the praise of the whole of creation offered to its Creator. Man's first and ultimate vocation is to give an intelligible form to this universal praise, and the liturgy of the Church, the Daily Office in particular, expresses this above all. Through the Daily Office the Church unceasingly continues this expression of praise offered by the whole creation consciously or unconsciously, in spite of being enslaved to sin.*[5]

Our difficulty in accepting the truth in this statement is that the prayer of the Hours has not been our experience; for centuries, the Liturgy of the Hours has been the preserve of religious communities and the clergy. While most of the reforms mandated by Conciliar and post-Conciliar documents have been implemented, the mandate to restore the Hours as parish prayer has been almost universally ignored. The church's prayer is left sadly impoverished by this failure.

Of all the riches the celebration of the Hours offers us, it is a premier example of what we have said about worship. We shall look at the liturgy of Evening Prayer by way of illustration.

For those who have never prayed the Hours, and for those clergy and religious accustomed to the recitation of an essentially monastic breviary,[6] the following is an outline of a parochial celebration of Evening Prayer.[7]

SETTING: The people gather in the church and are seated in a space appropriate to their number; the seating arrangement is "in the round," or choir style; auditorium seating arrangements are inappropriate. A stand for the Paschal Candle is in the center; nearby is a place for a thurible

---

[5] *The Taizé Office*, p. 9.

[6] The prayer of the Hours was originally a parochial liturgy, but it was its monastic expression which has survived the ages through the Roman breviary. *CSL* called for the restoration of a parochial or cathedral office, as the prayer of the local church.

[7] This outline is modeled on the liturgy provided in *Praise God in Song: Ecumenical Daily Prayer*, edited by John Melloh, S.M., and William Storey: with musical settings by Michael Joncas, David Clark Isele, and Howard Hughes, S.M.; published by G.I.A., 1979.

or incense burner. The scriptures may be enthroned.

MINISTERS: Someone, a pastoral figure in the community, is chosen to preside over the liturgy; another is chosen as reader; a cantor or schola is indispensable.

THE LITURGY:

— When all have gathered, the Paschal Candle is brought in and placed in its stand. Other candles are lit, or electric lights turned on when:

— The presider, or an assistant, intones, "Light and peace in Jesus Christ our Lord," and all respond, "Thanks be to God."

— All join in singing an appropriate evening hymn.

— Cantor and people join in singing Psalm 140 with its refrain, "My prayers rise like incense, my hands like the evening offering," and some incense is placed on the burning coal. The singing of the psalm is concluded with a collect prayer.

— Another suitable psalm is sung, also concluded with a collect prayer.

— Psalm 116 or another psalm of praise is sung as a doxology.

— A brief scripture passage is proclaimed; several minutes of quiet reflection follow.

— All stand to sing the Gospel Canticle: Mary's Song, the *Magnificat*. During this, the Candle and people are honored with incense.

— Intercessory prayers are sung, concluding with the Lord's Prayer; the presider prays a three-fold blessing upon those assembled.

— A sign of peace is exchanged.

Although there is a scripture reading, this is not a service of the Word. It is a service of praise and thanksgiving, an offering of prayers, song, and incense. One comes to such worship expecting to give, not to receive: there is usually no homily; one does not receive communion. It is simply prayer of thanksgiving at the day's end. In this liturgy we stand before our God and confess our faith in the Lord Jesus; we make an offering of incense as a sign of our prayer rising before God.

Evening Prayer and its companion, Morning Prayer, are the "hinge hours" of the daily Office: they are the premier daily prayer of the christian community.

Mary's song and the prayer of christians

In the history of our faith community, one among us truly personifies what we have said thus far about worship. For this reason, the church has always held this woman in highest esteem and presents her as the model of christian life and prayer. When this young, unwed virgin was told by an angel that she would conceive of the Holy Spirit, she prayed:

> *My being proclaims the greatness of the Lord,*
> *my spirit finds joy in God my savior,*
> *For he has looked upon his servant in her lowliness;*
> *all ages to come shall call me blessed.*
> *God who is mighty has done great things for me,*
> *holy is his name;*
> *His mercy is from age to age on those who fear him.*
>
> *(Luke 1:46-50)*

In Mary's prayer we find the basic dynamic of christian worship: acknowledgment of God's mighty deeds on our behalf and our response: praise and thanksgiving naming God the Holy One and ourselves in need of God's mercy. So true is the Virgin's understanding of this that her own womb became the sanctuary of her encounter with the Divine. The mother of Jesus reveals in her prayer how deep was her appreciation of our stance before God and our place in the story of salvation.

The essence of the hours

The christian community acknowledges the saving mystery of Jesus to be the premier work of God's mighty arm. It is this deed in Christ which we remember, for which we give thanks, and which leads us to call out and praise the name of the Holy One in creation. This is the essence of the Liturgy of the Hours, and it is not something confined to a candle-lit space obscured by clouds of incense:

Like all liturgy, the Liturgy of the Hours is a corporate prayer—the activity of the body of the faithful. In liturgical prayer the individuals give themselves over freely to making prayer together—offering a personal, but not individualistic or idiosyncratic, prayer. To enter into the liturgical act means forgetting one's own concerns and being present to the prayer of Christ's own body. . . . All worship is directed toward the living. The Liturgy of the Hours is no exception. Offering God time spent in "useless prayer and praise" is genuine to the extent that that prayer shapes Christian living. Liturgy helps teach the Christian how to live, how to make all of life a gift offered continually and freely to God.[8]

The work of restoring the Liturgy of the Hours as the prayer of the whole community is no small task. This is due, in part, to our identification of liturgy with eucharist and the other sacraments. Even more telling is the fact that our sacramental worship forms all have an obvious purpose, while the Liturgy of the Hours, as Melloh suggests, is "useless" prayer and praise. It will take some time for contemporary christians, accustomed as we are to valuing an economy of productivity, to learn the value, depth, and authenticity of such useless activity.

To celebrate the prayer of the Hours requires not only our understanding of its ritual elements, but even more our deep appreciation of what christian worship is all about. A universal restoration of this liturgy as the prayer of local communities will signal our deepening understanding of why it is we worship whom we worship in the way that is ours as christians.

[8]John Melloh, S.M., in *Assembly*, Vol. 10, no. 4, pp. 245-246, published by Notre Dame Center for Pastoral Liturgy, P.O. Box 81, Notre Dame, IN 46556.

Chapter 2

Let's Stop Planning Liturgies!

When we speak of liturgy we speak of nothing less (and nothing more) than the prayer of God's people: people seeking communion with the Lord as they offer their thanksgiving and praise. We are speaking of those moments when the saving mysteries of God's love for us are recounted, celebrated, shared, and experienced: the communion of God's people and their Creator. The liturgy is "the summit toward which the activity of the Church is directed; at the same time it is the font from which all her power flows."[1] The liturgy is the source and summit of christian life as it is lived and celebrated in our own communities: nothing less than this is the "business" of those whose care it is to make ready for and minister the sacred mysteries in our worship.

This "business" is a serious one and leads us to make three bold statements:

1) Liturgy *cannot* be planned and we would do God's people a great favor if we would stop trying to plan it.

2) Liturgy must always be *prepared:* to celebrate liturgy without preparation is a violation of God's holy presence and a crime against those who gather to celebrate that saving presence.

3) Preparing for the celebration of liturgy is a ministry and therefore it is an *art* which each of us, as minister, is called to practice.

[1]*CSL* no. 10.

31

These three are serious statements indeed: the language is, with purpose, strong and without reservation. Scrutinize and consider the following elaborations.

Liturgy Cannot Be Planned...

Titles exert a subtle and powerful influence over the persons and tasks they describe. (Consider the difference between: priest and presbyter; mass and eucharist; usher and minister of hospitality.) How we name ourselves and our work can easily begin to shape who we are and what we do. A critical look at a title may bring into sharp focus the tendency for self-perception to become self-deception.

Many, if not most, who read these pages will have some connection with a task commonly referred to as *liturgy planning.* At first glance, this seems a reasonable title: the subject of our work *is* the liturgy and a good deal of that work transpires in the course of *planning* meetings, with a group of folks often called a *planning* team or committee. We often presume that if there is a liturgy to be celebrated then there is an event to be *planned.* Indeed, if no "planning" precedes the particular liturgy we often refer to the celebration as *un*planned.

Before the work begins...

Let's take an eye-opening look at how much of our Sunday eucharist is *in place* before any planning team swings into action:

1) Every Sunday mass will begin with some form of gathering/entrance rite; this will be followed by readings from scripture and a homily; the table will be prepared with bread, wine, and book for the eucharistic prayer; the assembly will be invited to share in communion; the celebration will conclude with a blessing and dismissal.

2) The scripture readings will be determined by the liturgical calendar and the three cycles of lections.

3) Texts for the eucharistic prayer; the opening prayer,

prayer over the gifts, and prayer after communion are given in the Sacramentary.

4) All dialogue between the presiding priest and the assembly is standard and known to all present.

5) A presbyter will preside over the assembly's prayer and designated members of the community will carry out the various ministerial tasks within the celebration.

6) In most instances, the celebration will take place in a particular and well-known area of fixed architectural dimensions, a place filled with simple furniture most likely fixed in place by bolts or sheer weight.

Given all this, why, in God's name, have we and so many others spent countless, often difficult, hours in this process called liturgy "planning"? Is the "planning" of liturgy a needless duplication of work already accomplished by the Lectionary and Sacramentary? Does "planning" consist of selecting music and scheduling ministers — this and nothing more?

Good news!

Before we all hand in our resignations from planning teams, let's take a look at the good news our investigation of a title has thus far yielded:

— Much of our work *is* already done for us when the liturgy team begins its meeting.

— There is *no* need to duplicate what is already accomplished for us. (Perhaps much of the frustration which "planning" breeds is the result of naive and well-intentioned efforts to reinvent the mass on a weekly basis.)

— Perhaps we've been working against the grain in the past: making more work for ourselves than was necessary and channeling our energy in ultimately futile directions.

— Perhaps we have discovered that "liturgy planning" is not the best or most accurate title for the task at hand.

Our purpose here, however, is not simply the discovery of a new title to describe our work; new titles are often deceptively enticing and seductive. Rather, we are more interested in finding out how the old title has shaped our efforts in the past and has possibly been the cause of frustration in our work.

The problem of "planning"

The label "liturgy planning" is problematic insofar as it leads us, in any way, to believe that our task is to *invent*, *devise*, or *create* the liturgy. All of these paths are dead ends. Worship is not something we invent; it is the given; it is our duty; it is something we do. Prayer is not something we devise; it is a relationship of *encounter*. Christian ritual is not something we create; it is much more concerned with what we do naturally: we *bathe*, we *eat and drink*, we *forgive*, and we *marry*.

We may protest, and justifiably so, that it has never been our mind, in planning the liturgy, to "invent, devise, or create" it. It is at this point, however, that we need to be wary of the fine line between self-perception and self-deception: what is "our mind" about things and what our practice discloses are often two different realities whose only unity is the protective umbrella of a title such as "liturgy planning."

An illustration may be helpful. A parish liturgy team sets about the work of planning eucharist for the Sundays of the Easter season. There is a healthy desire to somehow let the rich feast of the Paschal Vigil spill over to the table of the coming weeks. Question: how sustain the brightness of the Paschal candle, the joy of the *Gloria*, and the wet, cleansing freshness of the baptismal waters? Idea: incorporate these in the Sunday opening rites! But a cautious voice worries that the assembly will tire of the repetitious parade of these elements. Solution: on the even-numbered Sundays of Easter the Paschal candle will be carried in procession with the *Gloria* as the opening song; on the alternate Sundays the candle will remain in its stand, near the ambo; a hymn will accompany the procession, and the *Gloria* will be sung during a sprinkling rite before the opening prayer! Such an inventive device is less creative than it is cleverly manipulative — and it

34

is the fruit of "planning." The problem here is that the process has either (a) asked the wrong questions, (b) asked no questions at all, or (c) asked the right questions but with little understanding of them. The "mind" of all this was simply "planning," while the resultant reality is a hodgepodge of variation based on the assumption that the christian assembly will quickly be bored by its own major symbols.

The Sunday eucharist

As a title for our work, "liturgy planning" is simply inadequate. What, then, will more fully describe the task of liturgy teams? A few remarks on the Sunday eucharist may lead us in a more satisfying direction.

— Sunday eucharist is the weekly gathering of the church community for worship.

— At this service, the scriptures are proclaimed so that God's people might hear the saving and divine word and gather at the Lord's table to be nourished and sustained for the task of going forth.

— The eucharistic liturgy is primarily a prayer of thanksgiving to the Father, offered by the sons and daughters of the church with, through, and in Christ in the power of the Spirit.

— This prayer of thanksgiving is made in word and gesture, in song and silence, in sign and symbol, in solo voice and unison chorus.

— Sunday eucharist is the church at prayer, meeting the Lord in an assembly of word, sacrament and family — a communion, sealed in the covenant of the Lord's blood.

The liturgy of Sunday eucharist is the ritual encounter of the church with God who dwells in unapproachable light: Sunday mass is the meeting of God's people with their Lord at a common table. This sacred meeting is *not* dependent on our design or plans; it *is* and is *all* the work of the Lord and God's Spirit moving in our midst. If grace can be defined as the quality of our relationship with God, then Sunday eucharist is surely a particularly graced moment. This graced, sacramental moment is a divine gift offered to God's people:

— though it is we who gather for prayer, it is the *Lord* who calls us;

— though it is we who read and listen for the word, it is the *Lord* who speaks it;

— though it is we who offer bread and wine, these were first the Lord's gift to us.

None of us is able to cry out, "Abba, Father," unless the Spirit first moves us to do so. Only that prayer which is made through, with, and in Christ, in the unity of the Holy Spirit — only this prayer is heard by the Father.

God's Spirit moves *where* it wills, *when* it wills, *how* it wills. Although we are unable to *plan* our encounter with the Lord, we are called, always and everywhere (for this is our duty and our salvation), to be ready, open to, and prepared to encounter the Lord who comes to meet us. Unable as we may be to plan the graced moment of encounter with the Lord, we are *obliged* to prepare for it. Each person, and the whole community, is called to "prepare the way of the Lord" and to make straight the paths along which we encounter the divine Traveler.

This brings us to a new title for the work of liturgy teams. Let's stop "planning liturgies" and let's begin to *prepare* for worship.

Liturgy Must Always Be Prepared...

To celebrate the liturgy without preparation is a violation of God's holy presence and a crime against those who gather to celebrate that presence. This language has been chosen carefully and deliberately, with the hope that we will begin to see that the difference between the terms "planning" and "preparing" is neither capricious nor marginal, and all much more than a question of semantics.

To say that *un*prepared liturgy is "a violation of God's holy presence" is to acknowledge that the liturgical act is an awesome rite indeed: in the liturgy, we discover ourselves in the presence of the Most High God; we find ourselves on holy ground but, unlike Moses, we tread that ground with feet shod and come face to face with the living God. We speak freely that name which the high priest in Israel spoke but once a year: we name the Lord whose own we have been named. We look into the eyes of the Lord and we do not die — we live! The color of these remarks is unabashedly Byzantine; we in the Latin rite might do well to study the spirit which our brothers and sisters in the Eastern rites offer their worship.

A sacred trust

Unprepared celebration of the liturgy is a crime against those who gather to celebrate God's holy presence. . . . In the christian scheme of things members of the community depend and rely on one another to minister to the community's needs. Those who assume positions of service in the community (certainly including those who prepare for the church's prayer) assume the *responsibilities* of those positions. Those who serve are given a sacred trust by those whom they serve; those who prepare and minister the liturgy are entrusted with the moments when the church will enter ritually and tread on that holy ground which is the Lord's.

Because that holy ground is the Lord's, the task entrusted to us (preparation of worship) is a sacred one and to approach that task with less than awe is to trivialize the ministry and to violate the community's trust: this is nothing less than crime in the highest of all courts. The work at stake here is intimately bound up with that which is our duty and our salvation. Liturgy teams and ministers are charged with preparing a time, a place, and a table for the graced encounter of God and God's people. It is the task, the ministry, of the liturgy team to:

— prepare a place where the community gathers for worship; to ready that holy ground, that house of God's people where Creator and created meet.

— prepare for the proclamation of the scriptures so that

the gathered assembly might hear the Lord's saving word.

— prepare the music of praise and prayer so that all might join in singing the divine canticle of the One who saves us.

— prepare the table and the table prayer so that all might join in offering thanks to the Lord who sups with sinners.

— prepare bread and wine, a simple meal, so that all might be nourished by the bread of angels and the cup of salvation.

— prepare a moment that invites the community to prayer and helps ready believers for communion with the Lord and one another.

Liturgy cannot be planned...liturgy must always be prepared: a ministry of preparation, of making ready. While *planning* liturgy may be a misguided and frustrating experience it is a relatively easy task when seen against the alternative of *preparing* for worship. This ministry of preparing is no simple task; it is a craft, and this brings us to our third area of concern.

A Ministry, And Therefore An Art...

The ministry of *preparing* for worship will call forth time, energy, patience, understanding, and much prayer; at times it will draw on creativity and ingenuity. In all of this, the work must be *discreet*, and ordered toward the service of God and God's people at prayer. The discreetness here is of the kind that prepares a truly successful dinner party where the guests easily enjoy one another and the meal; where each detail, large and small alike, contributes to the whole event; where the graciousness of the evening covers any breach of etiquette; where the host is responsible for everything and yet appears to be concerned only with enjoying the repast along with gathered friends. This is an art![2]

The ministry of preparing for worship is an art, too, for like art:

— it is modest, as modest as the art of living *with* and not *above* one's neighbor,

— it is basic, as basic as the art of knowing when to serve others and when to allow oneself to *be served* by others,

— it is crafty, as crafty as sitting at table and managing to engage in conversation with some flair while at the same time ingesting food through the mouth,

— it is indispensable, as indispensable as the art of learning and living with manners, manners that support, enhance, and enable us to strengthen the social bonds of graceful living.

The materials involved in this art of preparing for worship are simple and profound: faith in God; an appreciation for things whole, true, and beautiful; love of neighbor; and love for that heritage of prayer which is ours as christians. Like all good art, this liturgical art is not self-interested and is never self-indulgent. It is ever an act of love, a service done for the glory of God and the good of others. Like fine art, this liturgical artistry is *useless,* which is to say that it has no orientation toward productivity; it neither seeks nor expects compensation of any kind, for the doing of the art is its own reward.

The discipline of beauty

Such artistry is neither abstract nor obscure. It is practiced and struggles to flourish in communities of real people who fashion false idols and often forget their manners. We fail often for we are more practiced in the art of pleasing and

[2]I am indebted here to Aidan Kavanagh's wisdom in his major address to the Annual Conference of the Notre Dame Center for Pastoral Liturgy in 1977. The talk is available on tape through N.C.R. Publishing Co., Kansas City, MO 64141.

satisfying ourselves than we are practiced in the discipline of true beauty. The discipline of things beautiful is not something which comes "naturally" to us; the naturalness fell apart when we prized the apple of power and knowledge over the rest of Eden's fruit. We need to rehearse the right and mannered order of things; we need to gather, often, in a posture of praise in the Creator's holy presence; we need to learn to dance upon that holy ground with measured and graceful step; to speak the name of the Holy One with hushed reverence and joyful shouts — and we need to do all of this through, with, and in Christ, the first fruits of that new and redeemed creation.

While the title, "preparing for worship," may focus more clearly on the work that is ours and channel more effectively the time and energy we invest, it also challenges us to a deeper level of involvement. "Preparing for liturgy" is not a skill to be learned; it is an art whose subtle craft is intuited, discovered, and matured in the context of the church's life and prayer. Knowledge of and an appreciation for the tradition of that prayer's history is the indispensable honing of this craft. This is the tradition which the contemporary community maintains with fidelity, celebrates with freshness, and hands on to the next generation with hope. This notion of worship and its preparation flourishes in the hands of artists and dies in the hands of practitioners.

Patron Saints For Those Who Prepare For Worship...

In addition to everything else we have said in this chapter, there is one final argument. There is no scriptural basis for the "liturgy planning team." Luke's gospel, however, offers us Peter and John as models or patrons for those whose ministry it is to *prepare* for liturgy:

The day of Unleavened Bread arrived on which it was ap- pointed to sacrifice the paschal lamb. Accordingly, Jesus sent Peter and John off with the instruction, "Go and **prepare** *our Passover supper for us." They asked him, "Where do you want us to get it ready?" He explained to them: "Just as you* *enter the city, you will come upon a man carrying a water jar. Follow him into the house he enters, and say to the owner, 'The Teacher asks you: Do you have a guest room where I may eat the Passover with my disciples?' That man will show you an upstairs room, spacious and furnished. It is there you are to* **prepare.** *" They went off and found everything just as he had said; and accordingly they* **prepared** *the Passover supper.*

(Luke 22:7-13)
(New American Bible translation)
(emphasis added)

Certainly, Peter and John had no inkling of what would transpire at that supper table and much less might they have *planned* what was about to happen. These two men simply prepared the room and the food. It was the *Lord* who gave himself to his friends in bread broken and a cup poured out. Peter and John ministered and their service, like art, was modest, basic, crafty and indispensable. Their work was simple and profound. Their service was neither self-interested nor self-indulgent: they acted upon the Lord's request for the good of the other disciples. What they did — to prepare a place — was no big deal. They had no illusions of grandeur as they swept the room and set the table — useless, menial tasks. The art of doing what the Lord had asked was its own reward.

The artistry of Peter and John is our ministry; the gift of Jesus at that table in an upper room is our inheritance.

St. Peter, St. John, pray for us!

Chapter 3

Speaking Of Liturgy...

The fact that 90 percent of the members of my parish are
college students prompts many outside the parish to ask if the
students are coming to Sunday mass. Upon hearing that our
church is nearly full three times each Sunday, those inquiring
often respond, "That's wonderful! Your liturgies must be informal and contemporary."

The students who worship in our parish love our liturgies
and often comment that our services are more "meaningful"
than the "formal and traditional" masses they experience at
home.

Those responsible for preparing our Sunday eucharists
might be puzzled by such comments because our celebrations
are grounded in the liturgical books (Lectionary and
Sacramentary) used in parishes everywhere.

The subject of our study in this chapter will be the use of
the many adjectives (traditional and contemporary, formal
and informal, creative) we use when speaking of liturgy. Giving some definition to these widely used terms should lead to
a better understanding of worship in general and the worship
we experience in particular.

Old and new labels

In the not too distant past, particular celebrations of the
eucharist were classified as *low*, *high*, and *solemn high*
masses. Such distinctions were eased out of our liturgical
vocabulary and practice by the reforms of Vatican II. What
gratitude we have for such change should prompt us, in turn,

to question the new, if unofficial, tags with which we often label our celebrations—formal and informal, traditional and contemporary. While such labels intend as many meanings as the number of persons who apply them, there is a commonly accepted understanding of these terms in American parish life that does make them the coin of the day.

We saw earlier how powerful is the function of titles in shaping who we are and what we do. Insofar as the labels in question are used to title our worship experience, we need to be wary of their influence on our liturgy. Categorical labels are good and helpful insofar as they rise out of the nature of worship. Categories imposed from outside breed problems and misdirect the worship we offer.

It is for this reason that "theme liturgies" are ill-advised ventures. The inherent and only theme of each liturgical act is nothing more and nothing less than the paschal mystery of Jesus' dying and rising. Imposing on the liturgy even those themes that relate to this mystery (for example, peace, reconciliation, service) is often a misdirected effort to force the liturgy to say what it speaks so eloquently already on its own.

How, then, are we to understand the categories of traditional and contemporary, formal and informal?[1] Do they rise out of the liturgy itself, or are they imposed from the outside? These questions are not merely academic. The potential problems reach critical proportions when criteria from outside our worship begin to shape the liturgical act *and* the worshiping community. This happens more often than we may realize and the instances may tell us more about our worship than we care to know. We are all familiar with parish communities (perhaps our own) that are divided into camps according to such labels: the house divided against itself (especially the house of prayer) can neither stand nor long endure.

---

[1] It should be acknowledged that in the minds of many observers there is little or no distinction made between these two sets of categories: what is informal *is* contemporary; what is formal *is* traditional. This quick pairing of categories, of itself, is cause for us to investigate the matter.

Traditional and Contemporary

Liturgy and time

In the first chapter I told the story of a wedding anniversary celebration, illustrating the wisdom of the saying, "Remembering is a form of meeting." Remembering (anamnesis) is at the core of christian worship and it can teach us something of the christian notion of time. The "worship moment" is always a confluence of the past, the present, and the future. This lyric says it well:

We remember how you loved us to your death
and still we celebrate for you are with us here:
and we believe that we will see you
when you come in your glory, Lord:
we remember, we celebrate, we believe.[2]

We remember what the Lord has done for us (the past); we proclaim the Lord who saves us (the present); we look forward to the fulfillment of the reign of God, which is already upon us (the future). When we gather at the Lord's table to celebrate the meal of the new covenant, "we do this in memory of Jesus Christ, our passover and our lasting peace."[3] We remember and we do what he did on the night he was betrayed: all of this is celebrated at the table that is a sign for us of that table in heaven where the communion feast of the reconciled will have no end.

To celebrate the eucharist, then, is to carry on that tradition that flowed forth from the wounds of the Crucified, that was prefigured at supper on the night before his death, and that lives yet in the sacrifice of praise that we offer. What we do at eucharist is as traditional as the Paschal mystery itself and as contemporary as the Lord who is present in the breaking of bread and the blessing of a cup.

[2]From the song, "We Remember," by Marty Haughen, copyright 1980, G.I.A. Publications, Inc., 7404 S. Mason St., Chicago, IL 60638. All rights reserved. Used with permission.
[3]From the Eucharistic Prayer for Reconciliation, I.

Traditional liturgy

To speak of christian liturgy as "traditional" is to border on the redundant. Our word, "tradition," has its roots in the Latin verb *tradere:* to give up, to transmit, to hand on. The divine service we offer is precisely this kind of activity. St. Paul's words to the Corinthians speak with eloquence:

I received from the Lord what I handed on to you,
namely, that the Lord Jesus
on the night in which he was betrayed took bread,
and after he had given thanks, broke it and said,
"This is my body, which is for you.
Do this in remembrance of me."
In the same way, after the supper,
he took the cup, saying,
"This cup is the new covenant in my blood.
Do this, whenever you drink it, in remembrance of me."
Every time, then, you eat this bread and drink this cup,
you proclaim the death of the Lord until he comes!
(I Cor. 11:23-26)

Paul is articulate about his "handing on" the tradition of the Lord's supper. Each time we celebrate the eucharist we do the same kind of "handing on," even if with greater subtlety. In the eucharist we continue to "proclaim the death of the Lord until he comes." Our liturgy itself is this proclamation and it is this, along with the preaching of the gospel and the work of justice, that hands on from generation to generation the good news of Jesus Christ, the glad tidings of salvation.

To celebrate the eucharist, especially as the culmination of baptismal initiation, is about as traditional as any christian community can become. At the tables of word and sacrament we rehearse that ancient story of God's love for creation and God's mercy upon those who have and would pervert what has been given us. What we do in the Sunday assembly is as old as the faith itself. In nearly 2,000 years the form of what we do has known many changes, but three elements have survived all our whims and fancies: the telling of the story, our prayer of thanksgiving and the sharing of a meal.

Contemporary liturgy

To say that liturgy is "contemporary" means more than that it is celebrated in the present day and age (*com* + *temporarius:* with the time). Liturgy is contemporary inasmuch as it reveals in our own times and makes present the saving mystery of Jesus and offers life to those who would repent and believe the good news. That the liturgy is contemporary is not something that depends upon us who celebrate it; divine service is contemporary precisely because it is primarily the ministry of the Risen Christ who sings his canticle of divine praise throughout all ages. As the presider prays while inscribing the great Candle of the Easter Vigil:

Christ yesterday and today,
the beginning and the end,
Alpha and Omega.
All time belongs to him
and all the ages.
To him be glory and power
through every age for ever.
Amen.[4]

We say that liturgy is contemporary because through it:

— God continues to gather a people from east to west so that a perfect offering may be made to the glory of that most holy Name.

— the voice and word of the Lord continue to be addressed to all peoples in all times.

— the reconciling ministry of Jesus Crucified pours out its healing upon those whose lives and hearts are breaking.

— the work of justice, accomplished in the mystery of Jesus dying and rising, is proclaimed as comfort and hope for today's oppressed.

— the Lord and sinners are together at the table today, as when the Son of Mary supped with tax collectors and prostitutes.

[4]From the Liturgy of the Easter Vigil, the Service of Light.

Our divine service is contemporary because it is the prayer of the One who was in the beginning, is now, and ever more will be — in the power of the Spirit of all that is Holy.

Traditional and contemporary

We have tried to define "traditional and contemporary" in a way that is faithful to the liturgy they describe. Here, as throughout these pages, we are making the effort "to return to the basics," to learn again the root meaning of the worship we offer and to understand its place in the life of the christian community. In light of what we have said thus far, we offer the modest thesis that worship in each community must be *both* traditional and contemporary.

It is the Lord, through the power of the Spirit, who makes of our worship contemporary liturgy. Thus, a parish community at prayer (and those who prepare for and minister in that prayer) have little choice but to celebrate a contemporary liturgy (as we have understood that term). In spite of, or with the help of our preparation and ministry, the Lord will not be held back from gathering, speaking to, reconciling, and justifying those who assemble to offer divine service. Of course, there is much that we *can* do to enable and facilitate the spiritual exchange between God and God's people at prayer; to do any less is a crime against God's people and a violation of that holy ground upon which they tread. The Lord will come, whether we like it or not, and it is the task of ministers to ready the people for the Lord's holy advent. In the gospel parable, all ten bridal attendants were present when the groom arrived; only five had oil for their lamps and... Well, we know the rest of the story.

In a like way, our worship must always be a traditional liturgy, in that it tells the story and gathers us to prayer and the Lord's supper. Traditional liturgy *hands on* the life of faith through *anamnesis* and proclamation. However, when the *anamnesis* is so hidden or boring that it becomes *amnesia*, or when the proclamation of the Lord's death 'til he comes in glory is little more than a muted whisper, then "criminal charges" may justly be brought against those responsible for such a travesty. Traditional liturgy "hands on" its life when the gospel is preached boldly and when ritual is celebrated with such strength that none can blind themselves to the mystery of Jesus dying and rising, breaking and pouring out himself in the life of the community and upon the table around which the community gathers.

The community that celebrates this kind of traditional *and* contemporary liturgy will soon find:

— that it is less concerned about what instrument accompanies the opening song and more concerned about gathering the unchurched into the fold which celebrates the opening rite;

— that it is less concerned whether the song during the preparation of the gifts is a Latin motet or the Shaker hymn, "Simple Gifts," and more concerned about what percentage of parish resources are allocated for the poor;

— that it is less concerned about how high the Gospel book is carried in the procession and more concerned about how the Lord's word is calling for healing of the community's wounds (*every* parish has wounds!).

This is admittedly a tall order and a great hope, but the divine service we offer calls us to nothing less. All this, and more, is possible in the company of the Lord, through, with, and in whom all our prayer and work is offered and accomplished.

The Popular Sense of "Traditional" and "Contemporary"

Having seen how the terms "traditional" and "contemporary" best speak to the worship question, we look now to the popular sense in which these terms are used to describe worship experience and style. Certain polarities will surface in the discussion as a case is made for a confluence of styles and for unity in the assembly's prayer.

Because of the broad range of experiences in American worship, and because these two terms are understood subjectively, simple definitions on this popular level are impossible. The two lists that follow are designed to help the reader situate his or her community's liturgical program in a context for discussion.

"Traditional" liturgy

American communities and ministers who believe the worship they celebrate to be "traditional" probably fall into one or more of the following groups:

1) communities and ministers who believe that something valuable was lost in the reforms of Vatican II
2) communities and ministers who find value in celebrating the liturgy strictly as the liturgical books direct
3) communities and ministers who believe that our worship forms must be preserved and that the preservation of these forms is easily threatened by variation from the norm
4) communities and ministers who believe that almost everything was lost in the reforms of Vatican II
5) communities and ministers who believe that what some call the growth of an "American liturgical experience" is little more than a passing fad, a stage we are going through
6) communities and ministers who believe that fidelity in matters liturgical is a sign of fidelity to the church, its mission, and its hierarchy
7) communities and ministers who celebrate according to the revised rites but in a minimalist fashion

"Contemporary" liturgy

American communities who understand the worship they celebrate to be "contemporary" probably fall into one or more of the following groups:

1) communities and ministers who believe that the reforms of Vatican II made a valuable contribution to

the life of the church and its worship

2) communities and ministers who find value in celebrating the liturgy in terms of the needs of the local church

3) communities and ministers who believe that the options provided in the rites (and some of local invention) help worship life to thrive and grow

4) communities and ministers who believe that no "real" liturgy existed after the Edict of Constantine and prior to the convening of Vatican II

5) communities and ministers who evaluate their worship in terms of what is suggested at the most recent workshop or convention

6) communities and ministers who believe that fidelity to the church's shared mission of peace and justice is of utmost concern

7) communities and ministers who reject out-of-hand any liturgical prayer, style or musical composition of pre-Conciliar origin

With the exception (in both lists) of numbers 4, 5, and 7, I suggest that the communities and ministers in all the other groups have a valuable contribution to make to our discussion. There are, in these groups, varying degrees of appreciation and knowledge of the history of worship in our faith tradition. Some err on the side of caution, others on the side of spiritual adventure. There are also several approaches to the church's mission and to the relationship of the local community to the church universal.

Neither of the two preceding lists is perfect or complete; they each betray certain prejudices. Some will easily raise objections to what has been ascribed as traditional or contemporary. But before the quick and defensive critique rises in the gorge, let us call to mind our sins and prepare to offer one another a sign of the Lord's peace and mercy. We form (all of us) the family of those who confess one Lord, one faith, and one baptism; one God who is creator of us all. Can we not make the effort to see what our brothers and sisters have to teach us before we raise and wrinkle a critical brow? Is it not past the time when we need to study one another's liturgical expression? How long will we be so proud as to presume that those who don't do it "our way" are hopelessly behind the times, liturgical simpletons who have not yet seen the light (our light?)? When we move to a new community or travel on vacation, how long will we continue to pursue that futile quest for a parish that celebrates "like at home"?

St. Paul's letter to...

What I now have to say is not said in praise,
because your meetings are not profitable but harmful.
First of all, I hear that when you gather for a meeting
there are divisions among you,
and I am inclined to believe it....
When you assemble it is not to eat the Lord's Supper,
for everyone is in haste to eat his own supper....
What can I say to you? Shall I praise you?
Certainly not in this matter!

(I Cor. 11: 17-22)

Indeed, there are divisions among us, and the divisions are centered on how we celebrate (meet to eat) the Lord's supper—and we should be more than "inclined" to believe it! What St. Paul would write today to the Church in the United States might well be a letter we would rather not open. We are at pains here not to nominate either traditional or contemporary liturgy as a candidate for "Best Style in Worship—1980's." Rather, the urging is that the best of each style be fused to create one great river of worship flowing through the broad landscape of American worship. We need to learn from one another.

In some communities, the whole of the liturgical schedule might be described as either "traditional" or "contemporary." In others, some celebrations are prepared to be "traditional," and others to be "contemporary." I suggest that neither plan is a healthy or pastoral one. There is the danger, in both cases, that the stylistic consideration, "traditional" or "contemporary," (in the popular sense) becomes a criterion in preparing for and celebrating the liturgy. It is a sad thought that what could lead the community to prayer and worship might be precluded on the grounds of arbitrary, stylistic judgment.

Leave all things you have

A personal anecdote makes this case with poignancy. Recently, a friend came by my office and asked me to suggest a song that his folk ensemble might include in a liturgy celebrating the vows of several women religious. I asked if he were familiar with Suzanne Toolan's delightful composition, "How Brightly Deep!"[5] with its lilting refrain, "Leave all things you have and come and follow me!" Unfamiliar with the piece he asked if I might have a copy of it on hand. I reached for a large red hymnal sitting on my bookshelf and he said, "Oh, well, we don't really do that kind of music." Having heard but one line of the song's lyric and none of its melody, he was ready to reject the piece because of the book in which it was published! We have, all of us, much to "leave behind" as we ready ourselves to join in the song which the Lord sings in the halls of heaven. (Let's be thankful that the Lord's canticle of divine praise has yet to appear in any one publisher's hymnal!)

Formal and Informal

As soon as one speaks of formal or informal worship, images of each are quickly drawn in the mind's eye. Before dealing with this popular imagery, however, a look at some definitions will help get us to the root of the issues at hand in this study.

forma *(Latin): mold, shape, beauty*

form, n.   1. *the shape or outline of anything; figure; structure, excluding color, texture, and density... 4. the particular way of being that gives*

[5]"How Brightly Deep" or "The Call" by Sr. Suzanne Toolan, copyright 1971, G.I.A. Publications, Inc., Chicago, IL.

something *its* nature or character; *combina-*
tion of qualities making something what it is;
intrinsic character... 7. an established or cus-
tomary way of acting or behaving; ceremony;
ritual...

formal, adj.   1. *of external form or structure, rather than*
nature or content; apparent. 2. of the internal
form; relating to the character or nature; es-
sential. 3. of or according to prescribed or
fixed customs, rules, ceremonies... 7. very
regular or orderly in arrangement, pattern,
etc.; rigidly symmetrical...

informal, adj. 1. *not formal; specifically, a) not according to*
prescribed or fixed customs, rules, cere-
monies, etc. b) casual, easy, unceremonious,
or relaxed. c) designed for use or wear on
everyday occasions; colloquial...[6]

Consider the number of bells that these phrases ring in our
liturgical context *and* that these definitions come, not from a
theological glossary but, from *Webster's New World Dic-*
tionary.

Of particular interest are the definitions that appear to be
in conflict with one another. "Form" can refer both to the external and internal qualities of what is being described. The
primary reference, for our purpose, is the internal. When
speaking of the formal-ness of liturgy, we need to ask what it
is that relates to the "essential character or nature" of worship
that gives the liturgical act its shape, outline, order, and
structure. This is not to argue that worship should be formal
but simply to acknowledge that there is a *form* in worship
which must be understood before a case is made for formal or
informal worship.

Christ at the center

The *form* of christian worship is, simply, the Paschal

[6]*Webster's New World Dictionary of the American Language,*
(New York, N.Y.: World Publishing Co., 1960)

mystery of Jesus' dying and rising. Jesus *is* the "essential character and nature" of the worship we offer. (Recall that our worship is offered *through, with,* and *in* Christ.) All discussion of formal and informal worship must begin with this acknowledgment of the Christic nature or form of liturgical prayer and action. Even the assembly of believers that offers the worship is, itself, the *body* of *Christ*; apart from Christ, no true worship can be offered to the Creator. In this most basic sense, then, all worship *is* formal insofar as Christ is its essential character.

In the same vein, that which is *not* according to the form (i.e., that worship that is not essentially characterized in the person and mystery of Jesus) is simply not worship at all. In this sense, and at this basic level, informal liturgy is outside the purview of christian worship.

Keep in mind, here, that we are not speaking of "formal and informal" in the popularly imaged sense. The effort is being made, again, to "get back to the basics" of worship. All too often our time and energy (and squabbles!) are invested on the secondary level with no reference to, and sometimes at the expense of, the more important issue. The hope is that moving to a more primary level may help us to better understand worship in general and its attendant popular images in particular.

Formality and Informality

One way to distinguish the primary and secondary levels is to speak of form (internal) as formal and informal, and of form (external) in terms of formality and informality. Here the popular images are the stuff of the discussion, but not without further reference to Christ as the true form of worship.

Using the dictionary definitions again, we might understand formality in worship to be ritual prayer celebrated in an established and customary fashion. By the same token, informality in worship might be described as that ritual prayer that tends to depart from prescribed or fixed customs and rules. Our own post-Conciliar worship and its supporting documentation seems to encourage us in both directions. Certainly there are prescribed ways of celebrating the liturgy, but ample room is given, within some bounds, for variation, degrees of solemnity, and choice.

What the contemporary literature warns against is also found in the dictionary offerings: rigidity and the unceremoniously colloquial. When formality and informality become the molds for shaping our liturgical prayer then the potential for the extremes of rigidity and casualness are great — precisely because formality and informality override the inherent christic form, which makes worship what it is. What is at stake here is that meshing of the human and divine that is so perfectly accomplished in Christ and so easily and often ill-proportioned in ourselves.

Mechanical and trivial

Formality in worship may run the risk of becoming mechanical and less than human, and thus unchristian. Undue attention to detail in ceremony or the canonization of a particular musical genre may be at the expense of the prayer that music and ritual are intended to serve, not to dominate. Informality in worship runs a like risk insofar as laxity in details may trivialize the divine service to be offered. Canonization of musical genre is a temptation and danger at this end of the spectrum, too. While formality in worship may be uninviting to some, the personalization of informality may render the service inaccessible to all but an inner circle of devotees.

There is obviously danger in the extremes, but what of the midground? Is there not an elasticity within our worship that allows for a healthy tension between formality and informality? There is indeed, and this brings us to the question of *styles* of worship.

Styles of Worship

My parish is situated on the edge of Boston's hotel and convention district. Each weekend we receive phone calls from visitors asking for our mass schedule and further inquiring, "What *kind* of mass do you have at 10:00?" "Holy" and "Roman Catholic" are not the answers they are looking for. There is, of course, some cause for rejoicing in the knowledge that folks care about the manner in which the eucharist is celebrated. Still, we should be wary when people choose their community and place of worship according to criteria of style.

Styles of worship abound, and they accommodate the temperament, personality, culture, and faith experience of particular communities. This is all very much as it should be. It is the community's personality and life that enter the holy place to offer worship. Indeed, true worship cannot be validly offered except out of the stuff of our life together. All that is human bears the hallmark of styles: The most powerful experience of the sacred is to be found in the action of the *assembly*, therefore, we should expect that worship will *be* of a style. Nevertheless, when the community's personality (and its style of expression) becomes a priority consideration in our worship, we risk slipping into a spiritual amnesia, forgetting for whom our worship is offered, why it is that we worship in the first place, and how we offer that worship.

Style and authenticity

You will find here no argument for a uniform and universal style of worship: such worship would be inauthentic. Worship styles are terribly important considerations precisely because they are tools for judging the truth and validity of our divine service. It must be remembered, however, that a community's style of worship is not so much something that the liturgy committee members discover at a diocesan workshop as much as it is a living reality that rises up out of the prayer, work, and experience of the local believing community, as that same community is shaped by its heritage and its union with the larger church. In this way, the local community's style of worship is authenticated by the genuineness with which that style is expressive of the peoples' faith experience and by its fidelity to the history and current liturgical practice of its sister communities in the faith.

The most important consideration of worship style, then, is authenticity. Each community *must* develop its own style of worship, which becomes its own formality, which is to say: it is a form representative of who that community is and what it brings to prayer out of its shared life and work. At the same time, this formality in worship appropriate to the community must never become idiosyncratic: it must always evidence enough informality that the visiting brother and sister can be at home with the community's prayer. The balance between formality and informality is achieved when the community develops its style with serious attention and reverence for that form of worship that is our heritage in the rites of our tradition. In this way, the worship of the local church is ever in harmony with the church at large and the tables of Word and Sacrament are recognizable wherever we may travel.

Style and honesty

Each community is obliged to make a worship statement that is an honest reflection of its life and experience in the wake of the gospel's call and in its carrying out the gospel mission. All of this is rooted deeply in the Paschal mystery and thus the reflection of the community, which the liturgy is, is not only of the present moment, but one that also reverences the past and hopes for the future. Thus, the song of the worshiping community might well include old and even ancient hymns. However, such hymns are maintained in the community's repertoire not for the sake of nostalgia, but precisely because they continue to be valid and valuable expressions of today's community prayer. If such hymns fail to satisfy this important requirement, they must be dropped. In the same way, hymnody of all generations must consistently draw us to that vision of life eternal that is ours as we gather at the Lord's table. Lyrics that celebrate only the present moment are already passé in the christian scheme of things.

"Importing" worship elements from another age or culture, or from a piety or theology that our church has outgrown or developed to greater maturity is a temptation from which we should pray to be delivered. We must come to community prayer dressed in clothes well-worn by our life's work; we worship best when the lyrics of our song are scriptural or speak poetically the idiom of our life together in Christ; our thanksgiving must be in the language of our hearts and lives that we might grow to cherish the prayer we offer; and of course, the bread we break should be bread we have baked.

Style and divisions

Note that we have been addressing the *overall* style of worship within a given community. Authenticity in worship style is poorly served in a community that schedules, for instance, a "contemporary" mass at 10:00 and a "traditional" mass at 11:30 on Sunday mornings. Schedules of this kind are often intended to serve different groups of people in the parish.

Consider, however, the division in the community where one Sunday assembly worships in a "traditional fashion," and another in a "contemporary style" — by design and intent. If we cannot learn to sing one another's songs and if we cannot learn to join in one another's prayer, how do we expect to share in the Lord's healing and reconciling ministry?

Reminding ourselves that the ideal situation would be *one* celebration of the eucharist on the Lord's day for which the entire community would assemble, we can envision that a single Sunday eucharist would call for a confluence of styles, yielding a wonderfully woven tapestry of the people's prayer. Granted, a confluence of styles requires much work, time, and sacrifice, but anything less than this borders dangerously on remaining self-serving, self-gratifying, and self-centered — all of which is alien to the heart of christian worship.

Style and unity

Many parishes work toward this confluence of styles, once a year, for the liturgies of Holy Week. This is, of course, very much as it should be, particularly on those days when only one solemn liturgy is to be celebrated in each community. At the Easter Vigil all voices, prayers, and styles make the effort to be one, each group offering its gifts and its varied talents, its prayer and its artistry. Unfortunately, the second Sunday of Easter usually finds this same harmonious community once again divided up according to taste, style, and preference. If the Sunday assembly is the weekly remembrance of that greatest and most solemn of all feasts, that "holy night (that) dispels all evil, washes guilt away, and restores lost innocence,"[7] then how can we justify, under the new rubrics of style and preference, the dividing up of the community that celebrated that Vigil of all vigils with one heart, one voice, and one prayer?

All of this is a hard saying. The intent is to prompt an honest hard look at the different ways in which an individual community celebrates the eucharist on a given Sunday. Are we working toward a unity in parish prayer? If not, what is the balance between authentic diversity and divisive exclusivity? The following list of questions may help in coming to terms with the issues involved.

— A variety of worship styles exists in American parishes and in those around the world; styles that claim, justifiably so, fidelity to the liturgical books. What are these styles? How are they justified? What has been our style (styles)? How do we justify them?

— Liturgy is the celebration of the Christ-event, which is the ultimate work of justice in creation. What connections are there and should there be between our worship and our community's share in the work of justice?

— In what ways might our community's worship be more truly *traditional* and *contemporary*? How might our worship be more faithful to the *form* of liturgical prayer (the Paschal mystery of Jesus)?

— How can we work toward celebrating Sunday eucharist in our parish as one people, praying and singing with one voice?

[7]From the Exsultet.

— What do we need to bring into our worship? Of what do we need to let go? Are we willing to pray for the gift to know the difference and to do what we must to offer a fitting sacrifice of praise?

These are difficult questions, not to be taken lightly or answered quickly. Our response, in theory and practice, may be several years in coming. We did not get this far in the twinkling of an eye! The work and effort, however, will be well worth the wait. To engage oneself and one's community in this process will not be easy and will require of us that which is at the heart of the liturgy — sacrifice. In all of this we need always to remember that ours is a sacred trust and we tread on holy ground.

Creative Liturgy

No discussion of worship, be it formal or informal, traditional or contemporary worship, will go too far before the notion of "creative liturgy" makes its way into the conversation. Most often, the word "creative" makes its appearance with "informal" or "contemporary." Seldom do we hear a service described as "formal and creative," although on occasion one might speak of a liturgical experience that was "formal, *but* creative." There is a presumption at work here that deserves our notice and it is this: "creative" liturgy must be celebrated in an informal style precisely because it is presumed that "creative" worship somehow violates (if only benignly) the given "form" of a particular celebration. The corollary is that worship "by the book" does not admit of creativity.

Since the word "creative" enjoys an etymological kinship with the words Creator and creation, it might be worth our while to investigate its meaning as we pursue the issue of creative liturgy.

When speaking of "creative liturgy" we often intend some form of worship marked by the unusual or by some novelty. While dictionary definitions would support this use of the word "creative," we look, for our purposes, to the primary definitions: "having the power or quality of creating; productive of — ."[8] This brings us within striking distance of a simple thesis: all liturgy is of its nature, creative.

The Spirit and worship

All liturgy has the power of creating; therefore, all liturgy is creative liturgy. The tautology is intentional. We need to retune our ears in order to appreciate this understanding and to disabuse ourselves of the notion that "creative" has something to do principally with novelty or departure from the norm. To get at the root of creative liturgy we turn our attention to that member of the Trinity who has been given short shrift thus far in these pages: the Spirit of all that is Holy.

Let your Spirit come upon these gifts
to make them holy. . .
And so Father, we bring you these gifts.
We ask you to make them holy by the power of your
Spirit. . .
Grant that we, who are nourished by his body and blood
may be filled with his Holy Spirit
and become one body, one spirit in Christ.
Father, may this Holy Spirit sanctify these offerings.
Lord. . . by your Holy Spirit
gather all who share this bread and wine
into the one body of Christ, a living sacrifice of praise.[9]

Because it is our duty and our salvation, we offer praise and thanksgiving to the Father, through, with, and in Christ, *in the power of the Holy Spirit.* What would be our prayer apart from the gift of God's Spirit? No one of us cries out, "Abba, Father!" unless first the Spirit moves us to do so (Romans 8:15). Every lifting of the heart, mind, and soul to God is prompted by the Spirit; even the plea we make for help when we cannot pray is at the urging of the Spirit. This urging is ever upon us, never ceasing, probing always even the hardest and

[8]*Webster's New World Dictionary of the American Language.*
[9]From the Eucharistic Prayers of the Roman Missal.

62

coldest of hearts. The Spirit moves when it wills, where it wills, and how it wills: always and everywhere.

While each of us has known the subtle, and not so subtle, ways in which the Spirit moves in our own lives, it may be difficult for us to see how it is that this same Spirit moves the *community* to prayer. The work of the Spirit is often a surprise, it comes when we least expect it and in unexpected ways. The community's prayer is seldom a surprise to us: it is a scheduled event, announced in the parish bulletin. We come to this prayer for reasons that vary in their degrees of sincerity and sanctity: church law; custom and tradition; peer or family pressure; ministerial schedules; the desire to worship. I do not want to preclude or presume the Spirit's guidance in the work of those who plan the schedule of parish prayer; nor do I suggest that the Spirit works overtime on Sunday mornings, rousing sleepy christians from their well-deserved slumber and whispering in their ears, "It's time to praise your God!" What I do suggest is that the Spirit moves mightily in the heart of that assembly that gathers for prayer, as it does for the eucharist on the Lord's day.

Gift and pledge

If you love me
and obey the commands I give you,
I will ask the Father
and he will give you another Paraclete —
to be with you always:
*   the Spirit of truth,*
whom the world cannot accept,
since it neither sees him
nor recognizes him;
but you can recognize him
because he remains with you
and will be within you.

(John 14:15-17)

At a table in an upper room, moments before his betrayal, Jesus makes this promise to the church. We are promised the Spirit of truth whose coming we will recognize among us and

63

within us. The pledge of the gift of the Spirit has been faithfully kept; what remains to be seen is our ability to recognize this gift in our midst.

While the gathering of the Sunday assembly may be attributed to custom, schedule, and/or the Spirit, *only* the Spirit can be held accountable for the prayer which is offered once the parish is assembled. No *assembly* cries out, "Abba, Father!" unless first the Spirit moves it to do so. *Only* the power of the Spirit is strong enough to encourage and enable us to tread that holy ground that is the Creator's sanctuary of encounter with creation. *Only* the Spirit of truth empowers us to assume that stance that is ours before God: the stance of the empty-handed who come to offer thanks and to pay the debt that is paid already by the One to whom we owe so much.

— It is the Spirit who helps us to see that in the opening rite we gather not as the crowd of the bus stop or local theatre but as the people of God.

— It is the Spirit who opens the ears of our hearts and minds so that in the Liturgy of the Word we hear more than "readings": we hear the voice of God who speaks a saving and mercy-filled word.

— It is the Spirit of the Risen Christ who does the work of uniting us, in the eucharistic prayer, in that canticle of divine praise that Jesus sings forever in the halls of heaven.

— It is the Spirit of our Crucified and Risen Brother who helps us to recognize in the breaking of bread and in the blessing of a cup, the body and blood of the One broken and poured out for us so that we might have life and have it to the full.

— It is the Spirit of God who helps us to believe, in our unbelief, that "we, though many throughout the world, we are one body in this one Lord."[10]

[10]From "One Bread, One Body" by John Foley, S.J., copyright 1978, North American Liturgy Resources, Phoenix, AZ. All rights reserved. Used with permission.

— It is the Spirit who sends us from this holy table to
 live and work in that world which does not accept
 (because it does not recognize) the Spirit of truth
 who missions us.

Without the power of the Spirit, our Sunday assembly would
be an inane exercise in ritualistic, ceremonial behavior —
which is just what it may appear to be to those who do not
recognize the Paraclete. The question of the moment for ourselves is this: have we who *do* recognize the gift of the Spirit
in our individual lives come to recognize the gift of this same
Spirit in our communal life? This is another instance where
we have much to learn from our brothers and sisters in the
Oriental rites. We might take a few cues, too, from those in
the charismatic renewal who so joyfully revel in the Spirit's
gifts.

The Holy Spirit is the life force in our liturgical prayer, and
understanding and appreciating this role is of paramount import to those who offer divine service. Our worship *is* the
work of the promised Paraclete among us and within us. As
worshiping families we are in dire need of catechesis on this
point. As those who prepare for and minister in the liturgical
act, we need to develop a working knowledge of and relationship with this divine Ally who comes to make our yoke
easy and our burden light.

All liturgy is creative

It is under the sheltering mantle of the Holy Spirit that we
proffer the thesis: all liturgy, of its nature, is *creative*. That is
to say: all liturgy, of its nature, has the power or quality of
creating; it is productive. The indwelling Spirit has the power
of fashioning and shaping us as the people of God; we who
struggle to establish ourselves as committees would have no
hope of forming ourselves as God's people, save the Spirit
who breathes in us (in-spires us to) a life that is pure gift. We
are gathered by, and in the power of, the Spirit to be nourished by our communion with one another and the Lord, in
the word, and in the bread and cup of life. We do not "plan"
such encounters but we would do well to "prepare" for them.

Truly "creative" liturgy has little to do with novelty or variation in ritual. If there is any novelty to be considered, it is nothing more and nothing less than the novelty of how God's Spirit may choose to move among us in a particular time and place, in a particular celebration. Such novelty cannot be planned or designed because it is always a surprise. This is not unrelated to the surprise of the liturgy team when, after what they have deemed to be a disastrous celebration, parishioners leave the church thanking them for a liturgy that truly touched their lives.

The liturgy team and creative liturgy

Should we then scrap the liturgy team and leave all in the hands of the Spirit? The answer to this question is a resounding "No!" Creative liturgy, as we have defined it, is precisely the sort of celebration for which the liturgy team needs to prepare. This is the work of preparing a time and place, a word and table, a prayer and song that help to render the assembly open and docile to the presence and power of the Spirit in our midst. From the team's point of view, the task is to prepare that form of worship that renders the community vulnerable, as the created, to the Creator. In all of this, the team must remember that its work will neither guarantee nor ultimately hinder the Spirit's ministry among God's assembled people. A certain humility is in order here, which will serve to lessen any exaggerated sense of responsibility that the team may bear for the community's prayer life.

Creative liturgy is worship born of, sustained by, and open to the work of God's Spirit; any other notion of "creative liturgy" misses this primary and primordial mark. Communities that prepare for and celebrate this kind of liturgy will find, at least initially, that worship of this sort is no easy venture. To prepare for celebrations that are creative in that word's truest sense is to approach liturgical prayer with an earnest seriousness and with a patience for the Spirit's moving in our life of prayer. For a while we may pine for the flesh pots of novelty and grumble over our hunger for variation, but one Sunday morning we will gather up the fruits and gifts of the Spirit in our midst and that nourishment will be for us like manna in the desert.

Productive of...

The definition of "creative" includes a second entry which also deserves our attention: productive; followed by "of." How is liturgy, of its nature, "productive" and what does it produce? To get at the heart of this question, let us listen to a familiar exchange.

Mary: You know, John, I just didn't get much out mass today.
John: Well, Mary, you get out of mass what you put into it...

In light of our discussion thus far, what are we to make of Mary's complaint and John's familiar, if not glib, pious response?

What did Mary hope to "get out of mass" today? What does her desire to "get something" tell us about her approach to her community's prayer? Perhaps it is because we have spoken for too many years of "going to mass to *receive* communion" that we have come to expect that the liturgy ought to give us something.[11] Indeed, the liturgy gives us nothing less than God's own Word and communion with the Lord and the Lord's family in prayer and sacrament. Still, the liturgy is not constituted to be some sort of spiritual department store where we go to pick up what we need. The eucharistic liturgy is rooted in the Lord's last supper with his friends when Jesus offered bread and wine and *gave* thanks and praise. Our celebration of the eucharist is the remembering and doing of what Jesus did; what he did and what the Risen One continues to do eternally is to *give* thanks and praise to the Father who opened for the Son, and his brothers and sisters through baptism, the gates of everlasting life. Liturgy is first and primarily a time for giving, not for getting. For all that we can be grateful, we are thankful that, each time we give what is owed the Lord, there takes place a holy exchange of gifts and

[11]Compare with the dynamic of the Liturgy of the Hours as described in Chapter One, p. 26.

giving in which the Lord returns to us more than we can dream of offering.

A holy exchange of gifts

The dynamic in this holy exchange of gifts has a mundane analogy. At Christmas we are accustomed to exchanging gifts with friends and family. We purchase gifts for others with the knowledge that a gift will in turn be presented to us. But then comes the new friend in one's life, with whom the custom of gift-exchange has not been established. Should you offer a gift to such a person in your first Christmas time together? Will your friend be embarrassed if he or she has no gift to return? Throw caution to the wind! You are fond of this person and you want to express your affection with a yuletide offering. Have you known the joy of that experience when, upon presenting your gift, your friend returns the favor? Your new friend's gift was not expected; it was, like yours, *pure* gift, not a trade-off. Something like this is the holy exchange of gifts shared between Creator and created in worship.

Now, what of John's response to Mary? At first glance he appears to be on the right track in reminding Mary that she must "put into" (*give* something to) the liturgy. Unfortunately, there is a commercial equation in John's advice that might lead us to assume that John is, by profession, an investment counselor. The equation in John's response is that of the consumer mentality: put something in and you'll get something out; invest and live off of the interest.

John's response to Mary is based on an understanding of productivity that does not balance in the relationship between God and God's people as that relationship is celebrated and realized in christian worship. What we "put into" worship is not an investment that expects a return. At best, it is partial payment of a debt that leaves us eternally in arrears. If such "productivity" is alien to the dynamic of christian worship, can it be said that liturgy is "productive of —"?

What the Spirit brings forth

Recalling that liturgy, of its nature, is creative precisely because our worship is the work of God's Spirit, we must ask what it is that the Spirit produces. The same dictionary that defines "creative" as "productive of—" defines the verb "produce" in this way:

> *produce,* v.t. *(L.* producere, *to bring forward, fr.* pro + ducere *to lead.) 1. To bring forward; to exhibit; to show; as, to* produce *a witness in court. 2. a. to bring forth, as young, or as a natural product or growth; to bear; yield. . . .*[12]

These are the first definitions of "produce;" financial, manufacturing, and theatrical meanings are secondary and tertiary. Once again, the root meaning of a word brings us to the heart of the matter; liturgy is creative inasmuch as its life force, the Holy Spirit, is *productive* of our worship and of we who offer it.

The Spirit is "productive" in our divine service as it *brings forward, exhibits,* and *shows* what is otherwise hidden or ignored. It is the Spirit who opens for us the words of the scriptures and who shows us what is hidden in the gifts we offer. It is the Spirit of truth and justice who opens our eyes to the One who is our saving *Witness* in the court of God's judgment. It is the Spirit who brings us forth as the *harvest* and yield of that new creation of which Christ is the first fruits. The Spirit is "productive of" *us* as the people of God.

It is in this sense that our worship is productive and we can see that this "productivity" does not depend on some "spiritual capital" that we might invest. Once again we are reminded that we stand empty-handed before God when we worship. What we have to offer is already God's gift to us; what is brought forth (produced) is our need to give thanks for all we have been given.

---

[12]*Webster's New World Dictionary of the American Language.*

Chapter 4

Living the Tradition: A Contemporary Task

This chapter will treat of "traditions" and how they make their way into the history of our community's heritage. Much of what the contemporary worshiper thinks of as old or "traditional," was once, itself, new and innovative. The process of the new becoming old is ever with us and our own generation of worship is always leaving its unique mark on the ritual prayer that was handed down to us from our grandparents and ancestors.

Building Cathedrals

The cathedral at Chartres is recognized by many who have never visited France. Picture post cards and photographs in art books have made it a familiar sight. The most breathtaking perspective on this grand house of worship, however, is seen when approaching the small town of Chartres by train or car. Suddenly, out of the simplicity of the French farm country, there rises this inspiring testimony to the faith of those who lived in another age, in simpler times. One stands in awe.

My visit to Chartres was blessed by two very moving experiences. Their recounting here may help us to look at how "tradition" becomes part of the *tradition* of our worship.

Having walked around the interior of the cathedral for about an hour, I sat in a pew to pray. As a visitor, the beauty of the place was more a distraction than an aid in my meditation. One thought was foremost in my mind: this place was several hundred years in the building. Generations of crafts-folk and their families were born to the building of this church, knowing that they would die long before its completion. Our own age admits of few like experiences. Can we imagine giving one's life and trade to a project whose end we will never celebrate? One remembers Moses who was not permitted to enter into the Promised Land.

Sitting in the cathedral I looked up to vaulted ceilings and fine stone work, delicate and majestic in detail. I imagined a stone cutter who may have spent his life working a dozen carvings to be placed in a wall which would never shelter his prayer.

Then, even as the cathedral rises out of nowhere, there came from the silence the voice of music, songsters outside the cathedral, their hymn muted by the great stone walls. The song and its singers burst through the cathedral doors and the place was filled by some 500 young people who had pilgrimaged from all over France to this small village and its mighty house of prayer. Each parish group in the throng carried its own banner and these flags punctuated the field of pews in which they took their places. The aisles were decorated in the colors of back-packs, stacked like bushes with over-grown blossoms. Some musicians gathered just behind the presider's chair; a vested priest approached the chair and called the community to prayer in the eucharist. The already kaleidoscopic beauty of the place was refracted a thousand times over by the prism of God's people at prayer.

Generations of builders

What has the local parish to learn from this experience of cathedral worship?

We whose ministry attends to the celebration of liturgy are not unlike those whose craft helped the cathedral at Chartres to reach and pierce the skies of the French countryside. We are one generation in a long line of generations (past, and yet to come) whose work is to craft a few of the stones that help to build up the temple of God's people at prayer. The names of only a few among us will be recorded or remembered but our work is crucial: to make sure the foundations, strong the flying buttresses, and true the beauty of that shelter which the liturgy is for the hearts of God's people. We must know and trust the work of the generations before us, as surely as the generations to come will need to trust what has been our contribution. We must respect with reverence the original plans for the edifice upon which we build. To change the design midway through construction is to weaken what we build and place undue stress on a structure as delicate as it is strong. We must learn to be content that ours is not the privilege of cementing in the cornerstone: this finishing touch will be accomplished only at the coming of the One who is the Keystone.

In the meantime, we go about the work that is ours to do. We live and pray in the unfinished shelter that is our inheritance and we do what we can and must to bequeath to our children the beauty of what we have been given, hoping that we have added to, and never marred, what has been entrusted to our care.

Here come the apprentices!

Let us not be surprised, however, when the new generation troops into our shelter, singing its own songs, and "littering" the place with the baggage of its pilgrimage. This is all so very much as it should be! These pilgrims are our children in the family of faith. They are the apprentices in our crafts. They come not to destroy but to enjoy the beauty of our work! If they appear to be bulls in the china shop, then they are very much like ourselves in our younger days. How easily and quickly we forget! These are the new builders and they have as much to learn from us as we have to learn from them. They come with new tools and methods, new insight and depth. In our working with them the past and the present are wonderfully met and we find hope that the building will not come to an end. These new workers will make mistakes and their mistakes will often remind us of our own. We need, young and old alike, to be gentle and reverent towards one another as the heritage is handed on, as the task of Peter and

John "preparing a place to celebrate the Passover," is entrusted to new disciples.

The divine service we offer, much like the building of cathedrals, is both a traditional and contemporary task.

A word to pilgrims and new disciples

As the next generation takes up the work of building the temple of God's people at prayer, the temptation to change the plans midstream is a great one. The newest of ideas often appear to be without fault; time and history teach us a different lesson.

Our liturgical prayer is like a "treasure we possess in earthen vessels, to make it clear that its surpassing power comes from God and not from us"(II Cor. 4:7).The treasure is one of strength but it must be handled with gentleness, for its true home is the fragile heart of God's people. This treasure is not one to be kept under lock and key. Rather, it is one to be brought out for all to see and and to touch, in order that we might be touched by it. Still, it is a treasure nonetheless precisely because it is the communion of God and God's holy people.

We whose ministry is the liturgy do not *own* this treasure! At best we are guardians, or as the scriptures would put it, *servants* of this holy ground where Creator and creation are at one. The responsibility is a grave one and the trust is sacred.

I do not mean, however, that the builders of this generation will have nothing to offer for the building up of this treasure. It is to be hoped that from your own times and experience the liturgy will be embellished by the touch of your artistry upon it. Our caution is that you think before you act, and that you walk before you leap.

New "Traditions"

The history of christian worship is the story of how the disciples of Christ have prayed through the centuries; the story is traced by the mark that each generation makes upon our liturgy. For the most part, the treasure has been passed whole and intact from generation to generation. At times the worship tradition has been scarred or blemished in the process. The signatures of the present age will be many upon our heritage of prayer: we live in a time when a plurality of liturgical expressions struggle to be faithful to a healthy unanimity. Past are the days when those who went to Sunday mass would experience exactly the same liturgy in South Bend, Indiana, in Sydney, Australia, and in a mission chapel in Haiti: even the language of the celebration was universal. Liturgy now bears not only the stamp of the age, but of each local community, for worship practices and customs vary from parish to parish, and at times from mass to mass within one parish. In the future, students of the liturgy will have vast storehouses of Xeroxed documentation for their study of worship in twentieth-century America.

As servants of the liturgy, we are responsible for what we have received from our ancestors in the faith and we are responsible for what we shall pass on to our children in that same faith. Each generation, then, is a crucial link in that chain of prayer that keeps us united with that Passover prayer of Jesus in an upper room. Our responsibility demands that we take gentle care in how we celebrate the liturgy and how we fashion this inheritance as prayer for our own times. The divine service we offer is the prayer of the ages and the sacrament of that age of the reign of God that is come and yet to come. We who hold and shape this prayer in the present moment must be familiar with its history and its crucial role in the life of the church. A careful and studied approach is required of those whose hands shape and pass on the heritage of our liturgical prayer. This is as true at the local parish level as it was for the bishops of the second Vatican Council and continues to be for all national conferences of bishops. To help us to understand what is required in this approach, the following illustration is offered.

Holding hands during the Lord's Prayer

In many communities, it has become the practice at

75

eucharist for those present to join and hold hands during the Lord's Prayer. It has become a "tradition" (if ten years can be said to constitute a tradition) or at least a custom associated with mass on the Lord's Day.

Those who encourage this practice will tell us that the linking of hands throughout the assembly during the Lord's Prayer helps those present to see themselves as one body joined from its many members. It is also suggested that this gesture signifies that we are indeed one family of brothers and sisters whose spiritual kinship in Christ allows us to pray to a God whom we name Our Father.

On the face of things, one can hardly argue with the spirituality offered as justification for this practice: it is Christ-centered and ecclesial. But face-value consideration is not sufficient in this case: the gesture, in some communities, has become part of the ritual prayer of God's people, and it is not a gesture without significance. Holding hands with one's neighbors is not an element of the worship tradition that has been handed down to us but it is one that may very well pass to the next generation (or a neighboring parish) as part and parcel of how christians celebrate the eucharist. The reader may think this a minor point not worth our consideration but we need to remember that much of our liturgy's reform in the past twenty-five years was the work of discarding those "elements which, with the passage of time, came to be duplicated, or were added (to the rites) with but little advantage."[1]

How, then, are we to evaluate this custom of holding hands during the Lord's Prayer? We shall look at the origin of the custom, its intended purpose, and its placement within the whole liturgical act of the eucharist.

Origin: Our experience is that assemblies of worshipers do not spontaneously reach out to take their neighbors' hands when the presider says (or sings), "Let us pray with confidence to the Father... " Somewhere along the line a priest or other minister instructed the people before mass (or just after the Great Amen) in the meaning of this gesture and invited

[1]*CSL*, no. 50.

them to do it. Where the gesture has endured we can presume that it was initially met with a generally positive response. A few questions come to mind...

— What is to be thought of the gesture or symbol the meaning of which needs to be explained to those about to experience it?

— What are the implications of introducing into the peoples' prayer a gesture that involves the entire assembly but one not generally anticipated to be part of worship in the Roman rite?

— Does the individual worshiper have a legitimate claim in expecting that parish worship will be celebrated according to the liturgical books? What actions might be said to be an infringment on this claim?

A real issue here is this: some folks simply do not want and/or do not like to hold hands with their neighbors during the Lord's Prayer. Must they? Should they? Need they? In parishes where this is the custom, does the individual worshiper have any options? One can steel oneself against the exchange of the sign of peace (which *is* a ritual expectation), but one is harder put to break the chain of hand-holding fellowship for the duration of the Lord's Prayer.

Purpose and placement: If this gesture is intended to help us understand that in worship we are gathered as one people in Christ for the purpose of praising God, our Father, what is to be said of the value and meaning of the opening and communion rites in our celebration of mass? Are the signs, gestures and songs of the opening and communion rites so weak that they need to be shored up by the addition of this gesture during the Lord's Prayer?

The holding of hands is a gesture added to the many gestures already in the mass (standing, bowing, genuflecting, processing, sign of the Cross, exchange of the kiss of peace, giving and receiving of bread and cup). How does this added gesture blend with all the others?

Some argue that the exchange of the kiss of peace is poorly placed in the Roman rite; that it interrupts the flow of the liturgical actions toward the communion procession. Others argue that the Lord's Prayer presents a similar problem and would be better prayed as the conclusion to the General Intercessions. Does a gesture during the Lord's Prayer help or hinder an already problematic moment? How does the hand-holding custom relate to the kiss of peace? Have we considered the fact that one must drop the hands of one sign of unity in order to shake the hand just dropped in another sign of unity?

Finally: Suppose that one day, for whatever reason, it is decided by the presider and/or the liturgy team that this custom should be discontinued. How can this be accomplished without giving the lingering impression that the Lord's Prayer is no longer a community prayer, but now it is a prayer of individuals? Would the Lord's Prayer seem "less" when restored to its original proportions?

Drawing conclusions

You will have concluded by now that I am not altogether happy with the custom of holding hands during the Lord's Prayer: you are correct. But you should also know that I minister in a parish where this practice is the custom in two of our three Sunday assemblies. (Take a wild guess: how many "traditional" and how many "contemporary" liturgies are celebrated in this schedule of masses?) The custom was well in place long before my arrival in the parish. I make the effort to reverence what is, for many, a meaningful gesture. As much as I would argue against the incorporation of this gesture, much more would I argue against its arbitrary cessation on the word of a newcomer: just that precious and sacred is the prayer of God's people whom we serve.

All of this is by way of example. Questions have been raised to help in discerning the "traditions" that spring up (or are "announced") in local communities. Such customs will, for the most part, neither make nor break the community's worship nor provide a new chapter in the history of christian liturgy. This, however, does not lessen the import of our shaping the liturgy in local communities; nor does it free ministers and assemblies from the responsibility entrusted to those who are servants of the community and the divine service it offers. We shape our prayer for today with thanksgiving for what we have received and with hope for what we will pass on.

Thank God that none of those who built the cathedral at Chartres had any bright ideas about lowered ceilings or indirect lighting!

Chapter 5

Spirituality and Liturgical Ministry

This chapter concerns itself with spirituality and the liturgical ministries, including the ministry of the assembled believers whom other ministers serve.

The broader context for this discussion will be the experience of intimacy, and the desire for it, in our worship life. "Intimacy" is a live commodity in the business of marketing religious life. Books, tapes and retreats trumpet the value of, need for, depth, and experience of intimacy in the life of christians. The approach here will be more basic and less strident.

Spiritual Intimacy

Not at issue here are spatial or stylistic notions of intimacy in the worship environment or experience. Our concern is rather with the *spiritual intimacy* that is more an affair of the heart than of ambience. Spiritual intimacy may be supported by a particular environment or worship style but it does not root itself in anything save the encounter with our gracious, loving, and merciful God. Perhaps it is for this reason that the faithful elders in our communities, steeped in years of prayer and devotion, often adapt more easily to ritual and environmental change than do their middle-aged offspring: our elders root their faith in their experience of a faithful and saving Lord, more than in the trappings that adorn the community's celebration of that salvation.

The spiritual intimacy of liturgical prayer is born of those moments that we call conversion: the turning of our hearts to

God who made us, who redeems us, and who sustains us. We speak here of those face-to-face and heart-to-heart moments when the Lord's presence in our lives is unmistakable, unavoidable, and deeply powerful. For some these moments are few, but they are not forgotten. This experience of intimacy marks the difference between knowing *about* God and *knowing* God.

Worship nourishes intimacy

The liturgy does not so much produce or "confect" such moments as much as it nourishes and sustains them. The power of God's love, which draws upon our hearts, is not confined to or restricted by the celebration of liturgical acts. Indeed, it is this spiritual intimacy that draws us *to* divine service; it is that prior relationship upon which liturgy thrives. The best example of this can be seen in the stages of the Rite of Christian Initiation of Adults: the celebration of baptism is the sacramental and communal culmination of the work that the Lord began in the hearts of the neophytes long before they were admitted to communion at the Lord's table. Worship does not invent spiritual intimacy, it sustains and nourishes it.

This is not to downplay the power of the liturgical act in our individual and communal intimacy with the One who dwells in unapproachable light. In the christian scheme of things, the sacraments and the liturgy of the hours are the premier moments when God's people gather to remember, to find present again and to celebrate the saving deeds of the Lord in our midst. The intimacy between Creator and created in Christ knows its fullest expression in the church, the assembly of believers. Apart from the work and prayer of the church community, the believer is like the branch cut off from the vine, left to wither and die.

There is the story of the preacher who asked his congregation to not worry so much about the salvation of their individual souls but to imagine that they would be called to account as a *parish* on Judgment Day. Said the preacher, "If you live as a *people* who are to be judged, you will have no need to worry about your selves." The preacher helps us to put in context the relationship of spiritual intimacy to the life of the community and its worship.

Intimacy and maturity

It is in the intimacy of communion with other believers that we come to know the height and depth of God's love. Our individual intimacy with the Lord is brought to full growth in the church community; without the community's support and fellowship, we are undernourished. Spiritual intimacy with the Lord yearns to express and share itself with others, for the Lord's intimacy with each of us draws us into that people named as the Lord's beloved. True spiritual intimacy comes to maturity in the assembly, the work, and the life of God's people. It was through the *people* of Israel that the Lord was first revealed and it is the beloved *people* of the new Israel who are saved in the mystery of Jesus dying and rising. "You shall be my people and I will be your God" (Ezekiel 36:28).

The Pharisees' problem

The intimacy of which we speak is as inescapable as the Lord who calls us to it. The divine Lover who pursues and seduces us will not easily be put off. The embracing arms that seek us out are wide with mercy and strong with compassion. A look at the gospel shows that these same arms welcomed every sinner and outcast imaginable. Only the Pharisees seemed to stand outside the pale of this embrace: for them was reserved the Lord's anger and curse. Why? Because the Pharisees used the Law and its ritual not to free the people but to hold them bound, to load on their backs burdens too heavy to carry, burdens that they themselves would not lift a finger to ease. In particular, table and Sabbath laws were the downfall of those who could not see beyond the power of structure and style. We who study and exercise the law of ritual in our own times would do well to study Jesus' relationship with the Pharisees and his approach to the laws that they so "religiously" kept.

Intimacy and honesty

Worship demands of us and calls us to this inescapable intimacy with the Lord. The intimacy of divine service requires that we be honest as we stand as worshipers before the Lord who made and saves us. In prayer we find ourselves in the light of the One who is all truth, who searches our heart and knows our every secret. We intend, here, the heart of who we are as God's people, and the secrets we would prefer to keep in our family closet. When we gather for worship the heart of who we are as a community is laid bare for the Lord and all of us to see. A married couple may hide their problems from the sight of all, and even from themselves, but these same problems cannot escape revelation in the intimacy of their conjugal relationship. In much the same way, the hidden sins of each community may be closeted for six days of the week, but come the intimacy of Sunday worship and these same problems will reveal themselves, in a myriad of ways, in the Sunday assembly. Our sins of neglect, of infighting, of pettiness and jealousy, of anger and resentment and division — all of these are laid bare and made public as we process to that reconciling table of the eucharist, knowing deep within us how great is our need for the Lord's mercy in our parish family.

A fellowship of redeemed felons

Those charged to preach the gospel in our assemblies have an awesome task indeed. Nothing less than the preaching of the gospel will bring us to acknowledge both our sin and our need to be renewed by that intimacy that only the Lord's mercy can establish. We need to learn to leave our gifts at the altar and to go first to be reconciled with our brothers and sisters. As a people, the intimacy we share is the intimacy of felons who have been pardoned by the world's Judge. Through, with, and in the company of our Sinless Brother, who was judged and executed as a felon for our sakes, we offer praise and thanks for the great deeds the Lord has done for us. Pardoned and rejoicing, we are sent forth to minister the mercy of such intimacy with our brothers and sisters.

A Spirituality for Liturgical Ministers

Not too long ago, ministry was understood to be the business of bishops, priests, and those in religious life. All other work in, for, and related to the church was done under the title, "apostolate," as in the "lay apostolate." Came the 1960's and we discovered that ministry was everywhere and it belonged to everyone. We learned, at last, that ministry is the work appropriate to *all* who are baptized in the mystery of Christ Jesus: "If we have died with Christ, we believe that we are also to live with him" (Romans 6:8), and if we are to live with him, then we are also to *work* with him.

We speak of the "ministry of the baptized" as the primordial christian ministry. In the celebration of baptism, the one who anoints and seals with the gift of the Holy Spirit addresses these words to the neophyte:

Mary, born again in baptism
you have become a member of Christ
and of his priestly people. . .
The promised strength of the Holy Spirit
which you are to receive
will make you more like Christ
and help you to be a witness
to his suffering, death, and resurrection.
It will strengthen you
to be an active member of the Church
and to build up the Body of Christ in faith and love.[1]

Moments after we are born again in the waters of baptism, we are charged to take up that priestly work — the ministry of Jesus. We are named as witnesses to the whole of Christ's Paschal mystery: his suffering, dying, and rising.

Each of the baptized is called

How we live out this ministry of the baptized is in some

[1] *Rite of Christian Initiation of Adults*, no. 268, Provisional text, (Washington, D.C.: United States Catholic Conference, 1974).

85

way the same for all of us and in some other ways different
for all of us. The sameness consists in the work of all christians to give thanks and praise to God for all that is given us,
and especially for that justice that is ours in Christ; we live
out our thanskgiving by doing the work of justice in our communities, our nation, and in the world. The difference lies in
how each of the baptized is called by God: most to that
unique and intimate ministry that married life is, others to a
single life marked by a freedom to minister to so many in so
many ways; some to vowed life in a community of ministry;
and some to that ordered ministry of preaching and leadership. But in all of these, baptism is the sacrament that brands
the individual as one who shares in the Lord's ministry.

Particular ministries

In addition to these four major vocational ministries, there
are a variety of particular ministries in the life of the church.
Indeed, there is a tendency in our own times to name every
task a ministry. Consider those communities that have dubb-
ed their refreshment committee "the Coffee and Doughnuts
Ministry." In a church community where every activity is a
ministry, the definition of this term can become so obscure as
to be meaningless.

This is not to deny that the whole body of the church and
its life are truly ministerial realities and that each of the baptized is charged with the ministry of living a gospel life. But
when we speak of "the ministries" and intend an individual or
group set apart for the service of others, then we must
distinguish between those who serve and those who are
served. Neither is this to deny that the whole church community thrives on a network of ministries. Those in one
ministry serve their brothers and sisters in another, who in
turn serve those who serve them. Such complementarity is
the genius of our life together.

Why the rush?

The caution about naming every task as ministry comes
from a wariness of any neo-clericalism that may be afoot

upon the holy ground of our life with God. Perhaps the language is already too strong, but one wonders why it is we scramble to "anoint" all persons and tasks as ministers and ministries. Might we not puzzle over the fact that the ranks of the liturgical ministries tended to fill up much more quickly than the ranks of the justice and peace ministries?

For our purposes here the focus *is* on those ministries that attend our worship life. There is a certain ambiguity about these servant tasks and this ambiguity deserves our attention.

Can you think of any other situation, event, or community where:

— the *servants* make a grand entrance?
— the *servants'* names are often printed in a program that refers to the invited guests as "All"?
— the *servants* are guaranteed seats at the head table or in the front rows?
— the *servants* are the most visible and distinguished individuals?
— the *servants* are, often, seen *and* heard?
— the *servants* are the first to be served from the banquet table?
— the *servants* are the first to leave?

The temptation of power

Ambiguity abounds here and the potential for misunderstanding is as wide as the space in which these ministers serve; as long as the aisle down which they process; and as close as an apple dangling at arm's length from a tree in the middle of an ancient garden. Our first parents reached not for a piece of fruit but for the power promised in its picking. The serpent had assured them that if they ate the fruit of this tree they would be like gods. In other words, the ambiguity that surrounds the public service of the liturgical minister is ripe with temptation. As vice is basically virtue run amuck, so the minister's temptation to power and prestige is basically one's

87

service seduced by the desire to be served. In another though recent age we called this *sin*.

All this business about ministry is rehearsed so that we can begin to see how great a need there is for understanding *spirituality* in liturgical ministry.

Ministries and Spiritualities

The proliferation of "ministries" in our church is equalled only by its complement of supporting "spiritualities." Thus, we read of a "spirituality for lay ministry"; a "spirituality for the ordained ministries"; a "spirituality for social justice ministry". . . . The list goes on, though we have yet been spared a "spirituality for the coffee and doughnuts ministry." What we have said thus far about ministry prompts us to take a careful look at this plurality of spiritualities. If christian ministry is, at the core, a *baptismal* ministry, does it not follow that a spirituality for ministry is, at the core, a *baptismal* spirituality?

For example: the ministry of the pastoral musician is rooted not in the singing of one's song or in the playing of one's instrument, but in the musician's share in the dying and rising of Christ. The baptismal share in the Paschal ministry of Christ calls the individual to surrender his or her talents to the service of the baptized community. In the same way, the spirituality of the pastoral musician flows not from the particular service rendered God's people in the liturgy, but from the musician's share (through baptism) in the service Christ rendered us in the great Paschal liturgy of his dying and rising. The difference in each case is that the particular ministry and its spirituality are *expressions* of that root ministry and spirituality (Christ's) that belong to and oblige the christian through baptism.

We press this point for two reasons:
1) ministry and spirituality rooted in baptism of its nature, always subject to the dying and rising of Jesus and therefore subject to the church that is his body;

2) ministry and spirituality rooted not so much in baptism but more in a particular *expression* of baptismal commitment runs the risk of segregation from the community it wants to serve and from the broader gospel mission of that community.

To understand the risk in the second reason we will need to appreciate the value in the first.

A baptismal spirituality

Spirituality can be simply defined as the art and discipline of presence to the Sacred. This includes but is so much more than the quiet intimacy with God that one might experience in prayer or on retreat. The notion of "presence to the Sacred" is radically transformed in the Paschal mystery of Jesus. God's Word become flesh for our salvation renders "sacred" the whole of creation; to be "present" to all that is sacred is to be enmeshed with it, as Jesus in his suffering and dying was enmeshed with our humanity. A baptismal spirituality, then, brands and heals us with the sign of the Cross, the tree of new life. The fruit of the tree in Eden provided a temptation to grasp for power. The harvest of the New Creation is ours in Christ, surrendered and emptied for our sakes. Though we are bathed in the light of the Resurrection, our lives and ministry stand always in the shadow of the Cross: To paraphrase the psalmist, (Ps. 62), "in the shadow of your wings, we sing for joy."

A spirituality deserving of the name baptismal is one that renders us present to:

— the mystery of Jesus dying and rising in our lives;

— the Spirit who moves our hearts to prayer;

— the presence of the Risen Christ in his body;

— the whole of creation, which cries out to be reverenced;

— the poor and oppressed, on whose behalf we empty our selves in the work of justice;

— the mercy of God that is our peace and our integrity.

"Your attitude must be that of Christ. Though he was in the form of God, he did not deem equality with God something to be grasped at. Rather, he emptied himself and took the form of a slave, being born in [our] likeness" (Phil. 2:5-6). This is the spirituality of God's Servant and of God's servants. We do not live as our own masters and we do not die as our own masters, for while we live we are responsible to the Lord and when we die we die as the Lord's servants (cf. Romans 14:7-9).

As worship is our most honest stance before God, so baptism discloses the truth of our relationship with God in Christ, and orients us to that ministry that is the Servant's and the servants'. Baptism and the spirituality we draw from it are always ecclesial (communal) affairs. Though it is the individual who is plunged into the waters of baptism to die with Christ, it is into the waiting embrace of the baptized community that the individual rises with Christ. From that moment on, the individual ceases to live in isolation. The baptized are enmeshed with Christ's body, the church, and the mesh is one of mutual service.

In short, the value of a baptismal spirituality is its fidelity to that saving ministry of Jesus, which constitutes us as the redeemed and redeeming community.

Spiritualities of "later origin"

Ministry and spirituality rooted not so much in baptism but more in a particular *expression* of baptismal commitment run the risk of segregation from the community to be served and from that community's broader gospel mission. This is a strong statement and deserves some elaboration.

By spiritualities of "later origin," we refer to those that justify and support particular ministries within the life of the community. Such spiritualities are valuable insofar as they spring from a baptismal spirituality, as the particular ministry in question springs from the baptismal ministry. The problem arises in this way: in terms of our baptismal ministry we are all equals while the particular expressions of our common baptismal ministry may seem to separate us into ministries of greater and lesser importance, value, and esteem. What we easily lose sight of is that *all* ministry is important, valuable, and esteemed precisely because it is a share in the *Lord's* ministry. To be sure, ministries are different in kind, but they are equal in value because it is the same Lord who calls each of us to service.

> ...*I do not want to leave you in ignorance about spiritual gifts*. . . *There are different gifts but the same Spirit; there are different ministries but the same Lord; there are different works but the same God who accomplishes all of them in everyone. To each person the manifestation of the Spirit is given for the common good*.... *But it is one and the same Spirit who produces all these gifts, distributing them as he wills.*
> (I Cor. 12:1,4-7,11)

Spirituality and the pastoral musician

For example: the value of one's ministry in music lies not in the song one sings nor in the gifts that enable one to sing it well; rather, the value lies in that it is the *Lord's* song that is sung, and its singing is offered as service by the musically gifted to the community that assembles to join in the *Lord's* singing. Similarly: a spirituality of music ministry is rooted primarily in the pastoral musician's being fully *present* to the Sacred as it is revealed in the musician's heart, in the self-giving of the musician's offering, and in the community through which the musician offers back to God, with thanksgiving, the gifts received.

A spirituality for pastoral musicians (and all liturgical ministries) involves the "emptying out" of self-interest and self-esteem (dying to oneself) so that one may offer to the community what belongs to it. My gifts are not mine to give; they belong to the community that calls them forth for the service of God's people. This deeply are we enmeshed, by baptism, in the lives of our brothers and sisters. We are called to live as the community described in the Acts of the Apostles: to be of one heart and one mind. None of us claiming anything as our own; rather letting everything be held in common (see Acts 4:32).

Ministry: territory and ownership

The danger in the spirituality that devolves from the particular expression of christian ministry is its tendency to focus and even isolate the minister in that expression. When we name the gifts and the gifted we must always take care to name the Giver, and to be explicit *for* whom the gifts are given. *My gifts are not mine to give!* An otherwise wonderful experience of celebration and learning, the 1981 Detroit convention of the National Association of Pastoral Musicians (NPM) was curiously titled, "Claim Your Art!" One wonders who was to do the claiming, whom was the claiming for, and for what purpose would liturgical arts be claimed? Ministers who "stake a claim" on their ministry need to remember that the territory has already been deeded to God's people at prayer.

Finally, ministry and spirituality of origin later than that of the baptismal font risk segregation from the broader gospel mission of the community served. This kind of segregation is revealed when parish musicians are unfamiliar with or not interested in the work of the parish justice and peace committee. A few observations:

— It is not expected that everyone be part of every ministerial effort in a parish community.

— There are, however, elements of parish life and ministry deserving of the attention, interest and support of all the baptized.

— The works of justice, reconciling, care for the poor, hospitality, and prayer are the mission of the whole community and of its individual members.

— Some in the community are called to leadership in these gospel-missioned works, but the work of the gospel cannot be confined or consigned to the community's leadership. A working committee does not free the community at large from the work of that committee.

— A community of persons enmeshed in the mystery of

Jesus will discover that its several ministries offer the fullest service when they are understood to be complementary and interdependent.

This interdependent complementarity is not simply a coincidence; it is so because the work of all parish ministries (including those who serve the coffee and doughnuts) is *one* work, and it is one because it is the *Lord's!*

Liturgy and the work of justice

At the beginning of this chapter it was noted that the ranks of the liturgical ministries fill up much more quickly than do the ranks of the peace and justice ministries. This imbalance is one that should cause us to be concerned. We have much work to do in reminding ourselves that the Sunday assembly for eucharist is validated or falsified by how the community's ritual translates itself into the work of the reign of God through the week. The community that roots itself in a baptismal ministry and spirituality can never dispense itself from the work of justice, or peace, and of reconciliation.

Each Sunday we pray in the Preface, "It is right to give him thanks and praise. . . we do well always and everywhere to give you thanks. . ." This is how the International Committee on English in the Liturgy (ICEL) has chosen to translate: *Dignum et justum est. . . vere dignum at justum est, aequum at salutare, nos tibi semper at unique gratias agere....* A fuller translation would read: "It is right and *just*... It is truly right and *just*, proper and helpful toward salvation, that we always and everywhere give you thanks...." It is unfortunate that the Latin *justum* (just) was "lost in the translation." The members of the liturgy and the justice and peace committees, *and the whole assembly of the baptized,* would be well served in hearing and praying each week this intimate connection between the work of worship and the work of justice. The "connection" is, in reality, a *unity* because the work of liturgy and the work of justice are the work of the *Lord*; this work is ours too; we have been invited to "do this in memory" of the Lord.

Reflections for Liturgical Ministers

What follows is a series of reflections offered under the titles of those who prepare for and minister within the liturgy of Sunday eucharist. We name the "gifts and the gifted" not to segregate them, but, rather, to help us see how the many members are one body in the Giver of the gifts. Resist the temptation to skip to the section that refers to the service you offer, but read through the whole. The ministries are named not in terms of import, value, or esteem, but in the order in which these ministries touch the prayer of God's people.

We begin with a reminder from St. Paul:

In the name of the encouragement you owe me in Christ,
in the name of the solace that love can give,
of fellowship in spirit, compassion, and pity,
I beg you:
make my joy complete by your unanimity,
possessing the one love,
united in spirit and ideals.
Never act out of rivalry or conceit;
rather, let all parties think humbly of others
as superior to themselves,
each of you looking to the others' interests
rather than to his own.

(Philippians 2:1-4)

The Ministry of the Assembly

Yours is a share in the work of the Spirit of all that is holy, for in who you are and in what you do is found the most powerful experience of the sacred. Yours is the kingdom community whose very assembling is sacrament of God's presence in the world. In the living words, gestures, sacrifice, and meal of your common prayer, the living God is disclosed as the faithful and redeeming Lord whose tent is pitched among us.[2]

Yours is to be nothing more and nothing less than the body

[2]See *EACW* no.28.

of Christ. Yours is the ministry of being the beloved and espoused of God. Through your lives and in your midst the tidings of salvation are faithfully proclaimed. Yours is the work of telling and handing on the story of God's mercy. You are the people who embody the promise of life forever. For the world you are evidence that the word of judgment is tempered with compassion.

Yours is the ministry of celebrating again and again the Passover meal of the new Covenant. Your sacrifice of praise is a hymn to the Lamb of God who takes away the sins of the world. Yours is the work of gathering at that table which welcomes all who turn their hearts back to God. Yours is the ministry to bring bread and wine, to give thanks, to break and share the bread, to bless and share the cup — remembering Christ Jesus broken and poured out for your sakes. Yours is the proclamation of the *mysterium fidei,* the mystery of faith.

Come to your ministry from your personal prayer: it is the home from which you journey to the house of God's people, to the tables of their common prayer. Come prepared to be surprised by God's word and presence in the assembly of your neighbors. Come as you are! Come as sinners who need to find mercy, as the redeemed who need to give thanks. Come with all that needs to be healed, to the Lord who comes to heal you. Come with no expectations, save the sure hope of communion with the Holy One in the family of God's people.

If your community's liturgy is alive and beautiful, take care lest you begin to worship your worship: this is idolatry. If your community's liturgy needs help — offer it! Model your community's liturgy on Christ's divine service, not on the experience of neighboring parishes. The liturgy your parish offers is often a mirror of the life your parish lives: look into that mirror and see what you will see; then do what must be done.

When visitors praise and thank you for the worship you have offered, take delight in the blessing they have received, and rejoice in the work the Lord has accomplished through

95

you. Be faithful in the work you do, for through it the Lord saves his people.

The Ministry of the Liturgy Team

Yours is a share in the work of the Lord's Spirit who calls God's people to prayer. You help prepare the way of the Lord who comes with mercy and with peace. Yours is the guardianship of that holy ground where God and God's people meet and sit at a common table. Yours is the work of preparing the table of the Lord who is our Passover. Yours is the task of calling others to serve at that table, and of preparing them to serve with grace and reverence. Yours is the task of helping God's people to shape a prayer that they might sing from their hearts. Yours is nothing less than the responsibility of insuring that God's word is proclaimed, clearly and with conviction.

Come to your work from your personal prayer; begin your work together with prayer in common. Let your meetings be long enough to do the work that is yours to do, but not so long as to go beyond where the Spirit leads you. Root your meetings in the scriptures of the liturgy you prepare, for the prayer of that celebration will be rooted in God's word. Let your meetings be marked by a unity in spirit and in ideals. As others are called by the Lord, invite them to join in your work.

Remember that the treasure of the prayer of God's people is one you hold in an earthen vessel. Be gentle, and reverence what is entrusted to you. Let this treasure bear the imprint of your community, but take care lest it be smudged by your fingers. Should your zeal sometime mar or crack this treasure, do not panic. Acknowledge and study the error, remembering that the Lord will heal what you have broken; learn, as we all do, from your mistakes.

When your brothers and sisters thank and praise you for your work, take delight in a prayer that has touched their hearts, and rejoice in the work the Lord has accomplished through you. Be faithful in the work you do, for through it the Lord saves his people.

The Ministry of Hospitality

Yours is the first of Christ's faces to greet God's people as they assemble for prayer. Your greeting of welcome is the first wish that "The Lord be with you!" Yours is the word that welcomes the stranger to be at home, or the silence that makes of our assembly a foreign land. Yours is the task of discretion: knowing how to welcome, and when and where to seat the latecomer. Yours may be the last word that ushers the community to its week of work in the Lord's vineyard. Yours is the Lord's face and voice for those who enter and depart the holy ground of prayer.

Come to your work and your post from your personal prayer; be as ready as the Lord to meet his people. Let your welcome and your smile be for *all* who enter; remember that you will have time to see your close friends later in the week. Seek out the lost and the confused; do not wait for them to come to you. When appropriate, lend a hand and an arm to the disabled, remembering your own infirmities. Greet each person as the Lord, for that is precisely whom you meet. When taking up the collection, remember that it is for the work of God's people, especially among the poor; remember, too, that many who make an offering are themselves the poor.

Remember that you stand at the temple gates: some will come rejoicing, and others in fear; some will come healed, and others to seek that healing. Be sensitive, and welcome all as best you can. Some will rush by and ignore you: let go of your disappointment and pray for the Lord's gentle touch on their heavy or hurried hearts. Some may fall ill while at prayer: see to their needs as you would have them see to yours. Be slow to judge those who leave early: be glad that they have shared in our prayer and recall that only the Lord knows the reasons of the heart.

When your brothers and sisters thank and praise you for your work, take delight in the welcome they have found, and rejoice in the work the Lord has accomplished through you. Be faithful in the work you do, for through it the Lord saves his people.

The Ministry of Music

Yours is a share in the work of the Lord's Spirit who draws us together into one, who makes harmony out of discord, who sings in our hearts the lyric of all that is holy. Yours is the joy of sounding that first note which brings the assembly to its feet, ready to praise God. Yours is to impart a "quality of joy and enthusiasm [that] cannot be gained in any other way."[3] Yours is a ministry that reaches the deepest recesses of the human heart; your work is soul-stirring. Yours is none other than the *Lord's* song; you draw us into that canticle of divine praise sung throughout the ages in the halls of heaven. You help us to respond to God's word, to acclaim the gospel, to sing of our salvation in Christ. Yours is a ministry that gathers our many voices into one grand choir of praise.

Come to your work from your personal prayer. Let your rehearsals begin with prayer in common. Let your practice be marked by unanimity in spirit and in ideals. Be gentle in correcting one another: the kingdom will not fall on a flatted note. Open your choir to those whom the Lord has blessed with musical gifts; help the not so gifted to discern the talents that are theirs. Rehearse the Lord's song with the reverence it is due.

Take care to study the scriptures for the liturgy in which you will serve; know well the word that calls forth our praise. Let the lyrics of your songs be strong, true, and rooted in the scriptures; those who sing the Lord's word sing the Lord's song. Make no room for the trite, the maudlin, the sentimental. Open your hearts and voices to new songs worthy of God's people at prayer. Let your repertoire change as all living things must, but not so much that the song of God's people is lost.

Be ambitious for the higher gifts, but not beyond your gifts; respect the range of talent the Lord has given you and

---

[3]*Music in Catholic Worship*, No. 23, Bishops' Conference on the Liturgy, (Washington, D.C.: United States Catholic Conference, 1972, revised and reissued, 1983).

your community. Think first of the assembly's song, for this is the song you serve. Let your music be always the servant of the Lord, of God's people, of the divine service they offer. Let the service of your music always complement but never overshadow the people's ritual prayer. Let your performance become a prayer, and your art a gift. Let technique become no idol, but simply a tool for honing the beauty of your gift.

Remember that your ministry is ever an emptying out of yourself; when the solo is assigned to another, let that singer's offering become your prayer. When no one comments on the new motet, be thankful that your work led the people to God, not to you. When the assembly will not sing, be patient with them and with yourselves; the Lord's song is sometimes a quiet one and silence precedes every hymn. Waste no time wondering, "Do you think they liked it?" but ask at all times, "Did it help them and all of us to pray?" When your ministry leads you to music, it has led you astray. When your ministry leads you to the Lord, it has brought you home.

When your brothers and sisters thank and praise you for your work, take delight in the song their prayer has become, and rejoice in the work the Lord has accomplished through you. Be faithful in the work you do, for through it the Lord saves his people.

The Presider's Ministry

Yours is a share in the work of the Lord's Spirit who gathers us from east to west to make an offering of praise to the glory of God's holy name. Yours is the task of calling us to remember God's mercy and our need for it. Yours is the voice that calls us to hear God's holy word, and to share in the meal of the Lord's supper. You "collect" our many prayers and make them one in our prayer as church. With us, and in our name, you take bread and wine, you speak our thanks to God, break the bread of life and share with us the cup of salvation. Yours is to preside over the great thanksgiving of God's people in Christ.

Come to your work from your personal prayer; your public prayer with the community depends on this. Come to the liturgy steeped in the scriptures of the day lest your presidency be illiterate. Come to the place of prayer early; enter freely and peacefully upon that holy ground lest your ministry be hasty or unprepared. Come to your ministry as do all God's people: deeply aware of your need for the Lord's mercy.

Depend on and allow the other ministers to offer their services as they have been called to do. Let them be your fellow ministers, not personal aides or underlings. Be gentle when correction is needed. Remember that the liturgy is the assembly's prayer; because you are one with them, it is yours too. Call your fellow ministers to faithfulness and preparedness by the model of your own work. Ask not of others what you do not demand of yourself.

Let every prayer and word you speak from chair, ambo, and table be clear, strong, and true. Trust always in the Spirit, but not too much in your own spontaneity; even the poet writes many drafts before the final verse. Anyone can read texts; only the believer can pray them. *Pray* the prayers and *proclaim* the scriptures! Let all your movement and gesture be strong, graceful, and with purpose; the hurried step is distracting, and the weak gesture insignificant. Let nothing be affected; let everything be done with reverence. Handle holy things with holy care.

Let your ministry be emptied of self-interest. Remember that it is the assembly's prayer that you serve. Think not of yourself as the center of things but as the one who helps keep things centered — on the Lord. Let your eyes fall often on God's people as the eyes of the servant are on the hands of the master. Minister according to the customs of the church, and not by personal taste; this prayer belongs to the people and they trust it to your care. Let the liturgy be your prayer, lest the celebration space become your stage.

When your brothers and sisters praise and thank you for your work, delight in the rite that has become their prayer and rejoice in the work the Lord has accomplished through you. Be faithful in the work you do, for through it the Lord saves his people.

The Lector's Ministry

Yours is a share in the work of the Lord's Spirit who opens our hearts to God's holy word. Yours is the task of telling our family story, the story of salvation. Yours is to proclaim the true and saving word of God. You are the messenger of God's love for us. Your task is to proclaim that word, which challenges, confronts, and captures our hearts. You proclaim a word that heals and comforts and consoles. Yours is the ministry of the table of God's word, which feeds the hungers and the longing of our hearts for truth. Yours is to offer the story of the "great things the Lord has done for us," that we might turn to the table of eucharist with good cause to give thanks and praise. Yours is nothing less than the ministry of the Lord's voice calling out in the midst of God's people.

Come to your work from your personal prayer, praying that the Spirit will open your heart to what you proclaim. Prepare the word which is yours to speak: study the scriptures, understand the passage, let it dwell deep within you. Come to your work in awesome reverence of the word you proclaim: it is the *Lord's* word. Come to your ministry as one judged and saved by the word you speak. Anyone can read the scriptures in public; only the believer can proclaim them.

Approach the ambo, the table of the Lord's word, as you would the Lord himself: with reverence and awe. Handle the book of the Lord's word with great care: it is a tabernacle of the Lord's presence. Let your eyes fall often on the faces of the assembly: they are the body of the Lord whose word you proclaim. Let the Lord's peace settle in your heart, that your voice may be clear and steady. Let your voice echo the sound of the word, with conviction, with gentleness, with strength, and with wonder. Remember that the story you tell is filled with a drama you need not supply, but must always convey.

Like the prophet, you will sometimes proclaim what no one wants to hear; remember always your own need to hear the hard saying, and never imagine that your ministry places you above what you proclaim. If you are the best of the parish lectors, be gentle in helping others to improve. If you are the least of the parish lectors, seek out that help which others can give. If you do not know how well you read — ask: be grateful for constructive criticism and humbled by any praise your receive. Every lector wants to read at the Easter Vigil but not all will be assigned: be patient in waiting your turn and nourished by the word that others proclaim. Let no minister of the word think that there is nothing left to learn: another commentary and another workshop cannot but help the open mind and heart.

When your brothers and sisters praise and thank you for your work, take delight in the word they have heard and rejoice in the work the Lord has accomplished through you. Be faithful in the work you do, for through it the Lord saves his people.

The Ministry of Preaching

Yours is a share in the work of the Lord's Spirit who opens our hearts to the Good News of salvation. Yours is the ministry of the table of God's word. Yours is the work of breaking open the scriptures that God's people might be nourished by the food of the Lord's word. Yours is the ministry of Jesus who came to announce that the reign of God is at hand. Yours is the voice which opens the challenge and the consolation of the gospel in the parables of your homily. Yours is to tell a story that tells *the* story of God's love for us. Yours is the prophet's ministry among the home town folks. Yours is the task of announcing promise when hope is gone, love when it has cooled, justice to the oppressed and the oppressors, joy when tears run freely, and God when we are less than human.

Come to your work from your personal prayer, come filled with the word that judges and saves your own life. Bear the book of the gospels as the weight of God's judgment and the breadth of God's mercy. Bear this book as the ark of the covenant — with reverence, awe, and wonder. Proclaim the gospel as if our lives depended on it: they do. Proclaim the Good News as though we had never heard it: we are slow to understand. Prepare your proclamation of the gospel as carefully as you prepare your homily: the one will never fail, the other may be forgotten. Come to your preaching task ever mindful of your own need to hear the gospel message: when you do this, your word is clear and true.

Preach the *gospel*: this is all we need to hear. Pray for God's Spirit that your mind and heart be enlightened by the Light of Christ. Let your preaching speak to this age, but not be conformed to it; let your thoughts be transformed by the renewal of your mind in Christ Jesus, and we shall be re-created. Preach to us as people you have come to know; we know you so well by what you preach. Struggle as you must when preaching the difficult text or the hard saying: your honest struggle helps us in our own. Spare us the used homily when the cycle comes 'round again: our lives have changed (as has your own) and we hunger for fresh food from the gospel table. When the Lord has been sparing of inspiration, be brief: we will understand.

Let not even your own sin hold back from us the gospel's demands. Preach the word in season and out of season, yours and ours. Do not shrink from naming what is sinful—how else will we know our salvation? Preach sin and grace for this is what we know the best and need to hear again. Preach the reign of God in our midst: help us to know its signs and presence. Tell us the story of God's mercy: no other story does as much. Show us Jesus dying and rising among us: this is what we have come here to see.

When your brothers and sisters praise and thank you for your work, take delight in the word that has nourished them and rejoice in the work the Lord has accomplished through you. Be faithful in the work you do, for through it the Lord saves his people.

The Ministers of Danced Prayer

Yours is a share in the work of the Lord's Spirit who is ever moving in our hearts and among God's people. You gesture with your whole selves the prayer we know in our hearts: with us and for us you bring that prayer to living sign; yours is a ministry of Word become flesh. You move among us like

God's own Spirit: with beauty and strength; with fire and peace; with tenderness and power. In all of this you lead us, in the Spirit, to lift our hands and hearts in praise of the living God.

Come to your work from your personal prayer. Come filled with the song, the Word, and the silence of your prayer. Let the dance of your own prayer overflow in prayer and movement for the assembled believers. Please, do not come to dance for us; come only to lead us in prayer through the dance that is your prayer for the Lord. Prepare for your ministry as the preacher prepares for the homily: with time, energy, prayer, and work. We are not interested in your extemporaneous performance; rather, dance for us and with us the prayer you know by heart.

Understand that we will not always understand your ministry. Be patient with us, and help us to learn, to appreciate the wonder of all the gifts the Lord shares through our brothers and sisters. Teach us to pray with our whole selves, and be patient with us when we are awkward and embarrassed. Be gentle in leading us and our prayer, and the heart and flesh from which we pray.

Remember that your ministry is a giving of self and that your danced prayer is uniquely a giving of your whole self in the Lord's service. More than most ministers, you render your whole person and prayer vulnerable to our critique and misunderstanding. Forgive us when we sin; forgive our jealousy and pettiness. Do not wonder if we enjoyed your dance; rather, ponder how it has (or hasn't) led us to pray with you.

When your brothers and sisters praise and thank you for your work, take delight in the prayer they have shared, and be thankful for the work the Lord has accomplished through your gift. Be faithful in the work you do, for through it the Lord saves his people.

The Ministers of the Eucharist

Yours is a share in the work of the Lord's Spirit who makes of us one bread, one body, the cup of blessing which we bless. Yours is the work of ministering Christ's body and blood to the body of Christ, the church. Yours is service at the Lord's reconciling table. You name for each of us the gifts we have offered and the gifts we receive: "The Body of Christ, the Blood of Christ." You minister holy food to holy people in the holiest of all communions. Yours is the ministry of the One who was broken and poured out for our sakes: the ministry of Christ who is our Passover and our lasting peace.

Come to your work from your personal prayer, praying that the Lord will heal your brokenness as you break and pour out yourselves for others. Remember the purity of the gifts you minister and how great is your need for the Lord's mercy. Learn to love the eucharist you minister: let it heal the hurt your heart is slow to acknowledge; let it make you one with all that is living; let it help you revere all those whom you serve. Ministers of the eucharist are many; truly eucharistic ministers are what you must become. Let your service at the Lord's table make of your life a table of mercy and welcome for all you know and meet.

In and outside the worship space, reverence those you serve as you would reverence the sacrament you minister. When you minister to friends and family, remember that the greatest bond you share is in the Lord. When you minister to visitors and strangers, reverence them as you would your closest friend. When you will minister to those with whom you are at odds, reverence them as the Lord does you in your sin. Some will esteem you as "holy" because of the work you do: remember that your holiness is the Lord's work within you. When you are asked to serve at inconvenient times, let the needs of God's people be your first consideration. When you begin to think that your ministry makes you an important person in the community, remember that what the Lord did at table became a sign of the Cross.

When your brothers and sisters praise and thank you for your work, take delight in the communion you share with them in Christ and rejoice in the work the Lord has accomplished through you. Be faithful in the work you do, for through it the Lord saves his people.

One Bread, One Cup, One Ministry

There is much overlapping in the reflections we have offered. This is to be expected when we are speaking of *one* ministry (the Lord's), and of one spirituality (rooted in our baptism). Our reflections also all reveal some specificity precisely because the gifts and ministries are *many*. This is not to say that they compete with one another, rather they complement and serve one another as they serve God's people at prayer. In a kitchen, the one who washes the dishes receives less public attention than does the one who prepares the meal. Still, without the scullery help the chef's creations will never make it to the table. The service of both contributes to the nourishment of the diners and when either is absent, the people go hungry. It is much the same at the Lord's table and among those who serve that table. Value, esteem, and importance are determined not by the particular service rendered but by the Lord's service in which we have shared and through which God's people are served and saved.

Earlier we noted the anomalous situation in which the servants at the Lord's table receive top billing and front row seats. Although such attention may lead to misunderstanding, it is also appropriate. This is so, not because those who serve merit attention to themselves, but because the service they render is revealing of Christ's service in our midst. It is beneficial to the assembly to know that the baptismal impulse to imitate and incarnate the Lord's work is alive and flourishing in their midst. This notion will be clearly understood in the community whose ministers first recognize it themselves. As the community begins to name the ministry of lectors, presiders, and musicians as the *Lord's* ministry, it will begin to name its own assembled self as the body of Christ. The church, Christ's body, *is* the Lord's ministry in the building up of the city of God. The new Jerusalem is as near or far away as how the local church community enfleshes the dying and rising of Jesus who is its Sovereign.

The liturgy is not some theatre where actors on stage take bows and applause at curtain call. It is, however, that arena of holy ground where God's people stand naked and empty-handed in the Creator's presence. Our time and prayer in this holy place are served by sinners like ourselves whose only vesture is ours, too: we are all clothed in Christ as the new creation. These servants point the way for all who assemble. Their proximity to table and ambo is one of service, not priority. These servants are seen and heard so that all might see and hear the Lord among us. If they are the first to be served from the table, it is so they might be nourished for the serving of others. They are distinguished not so much by what they do, but by whose work they have become in its doing.

As we began, we shall conclude these reflections with the words of St. Paul:

I plead with you, then, as a prisoner for the Lord,
to live a life worthy of the calling you have received,
with perfect humility, meekness, and patience,
bearing with one another lovingly.
Make every effort to preserve the unity
which has the Spirit as its origin
and peace as its binding force...
There is but one body and one Spirit,
just as there is but one hope given all of you by your call.
There is one Lord, one faith, one baptism,
one God and Father of all,
who is over all, works through all, and is in all.
...and you must lay aside your former way of
 life and the old self
which deteriorates through illusion and desire,
and acquire a fresh, spiritual way of thinking.
You must put on that new man created in God's image,
whose justice and holiness are born of truth.

(Ephesians 4: 1-6, 22-24)

Blessing and Dismissal

There is a certain wisdom in our ritual for celebrating the eucharist that should not escape our attention. The best of opening rites[1] bring us with no delay to the table of God's word. Almost as soon as we have gathered, we begin to tell the family's story. The stories within this story are many, as they are in every family. These are stories of beginnings and roots, of life and of death, of hard times and how we survived them. Most of all, this is the story of that binding and merciful Lover who makes us one as family. Because this is the story of God's love for us it is promise as well as history and so it is the story of our future.

The story told and shared, we go to the family table that is ours because it is the Lord's. There is no denying that we come to this table to feast, but first we offer that greatest blessing before a meal: the praise and thanks of the eucharistic prayer. With one great "Amen!" we share the Lord's supper. The family gathering is now complete in the Passover meal of the new covenant.

Finally, and with a brevity the opening rite would do well to imitate, we pray for the Lord's blessing upon us and are dismissed for the work we have been nourished to do. There is a wonderful economy of time here that provides for the elements of our prayer just what is appropriate. In similar

[1]The "best" of opening rites are those that are not cluttered by the inclusion of several disparate elements: the rite that brings us together and prepares us for hearing the word proclaimed.

fashion, this discussion is concluded by a few pages of "blessing and dismissal."

Blessing

An old Latin "blessing before meals," begins with the words, *"Benedicamus Domino!"* or, "Let us bless the Lord!" We are perhaps more accustomed to blessing medals, food, and a variety of other items, than to blessing God. The blessing best known to all of us is the gesture of "blessing ourselves" with the sign of the Cross. The words that accompany this simple action tell us much about the nature of blessing. "In the name of the Father, and of the Son, and of the Holy Spirit, Amen." Whatever might prompt us to make this gestured invocation, its prayer text turns our heart's and mind's attention to the God who made, redeemed, and sustains us. This is true blessing at its best. When we "bless" persons or objects, our prayer should be one of thanksgiving to God for the gift of this person or object, which thanksgiving prompts us to call God "holy" for all we have received.[2]

We review this understanding of blessing by way of summary and parting admonition.

Back to basics

From our initial discussion of those basic questions, "Whom do we worship? Why do we worship? How do we worship whom we worship?" we have looked at liturgy (in particular, the eucharist) as one great blessing of God by the assembly of God's people. Liturgy is a benediction in which we "speak well" (*bene* + *dicere*) of the mighty and merciful God whose people we are. Christian worship is the way in which the community of believers is "signed by the Cross" while proclaiming the blessed Trinity revealed in the gospel.

[2]This is the kind of prayer that Mary speaks in her canticle of blessing, the Magnificat (Luke 1:46-55). Our Eucharistic prayers also reflect this "blessing" dynamic that has its roots in the *berekah* (blessing) prayers of our Jewish ancestry.

Because we stand as those in the world who bless the Lord, we have come to see the vital import of being *prepared* to stand in the sanctuary of blessing that the liturgy is: any other approach is deemed criminal in the halls of kingdom justice. We have made distinctions between formal and informal, creative and contemporary worship. We have seen that the truest blessing we speak is the one *conformed* to the dying and rising of Jesus; that the most honest blessing we make is the one faithful to the heritage of blessing that is ours in the Anointed One of Israel, and the one faithful to the Risen One in our own experience and times. Overall, we have said that blessing in the sanctuary of worship is validated in Christ and by our share in the work of justice accomplished in his Paschal mystery.

Finally, we have seen that the ministry of blessing God belongs to the whole assembly by virtue of their baptism and that a spirituality for this, and particular expressions of that, ministry is one rooted in, branded and healed by the Cross of Christ. We have asked those in each of these ministries to reflect on the service they offer as a share in the Lord's saving ministry on behalf of God's people.

In all of this the God-centeredness of our worship and life in and outside the sanctuary is of preeminent import. A reading of the signs of our liturgical times suggests that such an argument, and the strength of it, is not without value for those who worship in the American church. We christians are those who walk the path of Jesus, whose meshing of humanity and divinity is our salvation. If in these pages I have erred on the side of divinity it has not been without cause, and you are assured that my personal erring tendencies usually lie in the opposite direction.

Dismissal

The parting admonition is a simple one: take care that this book be for all of us an occasion for appreciating more deeply our celebration of God's mercy in the liturgy. Take equal care lest these pages become a tool for judging others, their prayer, and how they offer it. Presuming that the readership consists of worshipers, there will have been a tendency to read these pages in terms of our own and others' liturgy: at least this has been my hope. My fear, however, is the temptation to run back to liturgy teams, presiders, ministers, and choirs to critique the community's prayer. Before this book is put down, remember there is very little *new* in these pages; at best we have rehearsed a theology, spirituality, and liturgy as old as that upper room that Peter and John prepared for Christ's Passover.

Anything here that seems to be new is only apparently so. What may strike the individual as discovery may well be "old hat" to those whose ministry and liturgy these pages may lead you to critique. Keep this in mind: in many ways our communities have been faithful in the task of doing in Christ's memory what he commanded us to do in the Supper of his Easter mystery. In those areas where we have been less than faithful there is work to be done, but this work will not be so much accomplished by change in liturgical style or practice as it will be realized in the deepening conversion of the hearts of all of us. And that conversion, it should be no surprise, is the Lord's work in our lives.

Patience and Understanding

This is not said to stifle zeal, enthusiasm, or renewal among those whose ministry attends to divine service. Rather it is intended to temper zeal with patience, to infuse enthusiasm with gentleness, and to bless renewal efforts with a holy and wholesome respect for the prayer that God's people already offer. In this we can learn from our recent past. The turmoil in our church's life occasioned by the nearly overnight reforms of the early 1960's are a part of worship history we would do well not to repeat. The reforms, in many cases, presumed an expression of faith experience whose vocabulary was perhaps more foreign to us than the Latin about to meet its demise. Patience, understanding, and catechesis should have been the order of the day, and must be in our own times as the liturgy continues to be renewed by our study, understanding, and experience. As those who usually err on the side of our humanity, we must make the effort to see that our work, our prayer, and the service we offer are one with Christ Jesus, the Lord, whose canticle of praise in the halls of heaven is ours in every age.

Rejoice in the Lord always!
I say it again, Rejoice!
Everyone should see how unselfish you are.
The Lord is near.
Dismiss all anxiety from your minds.
Present your needs to God
in every form of prayer
and in petitions full of gratitude.
Then God's own peace,
which is beyond all understanding,
will stand guard over your hearts and minds
in Christ Jesus.

Finally, my brothers,
your thoughts should be directed to all that is true,
all that deserves respect, all that is honest,
pure, admirable, decent, virtuous,
or worthy of praise.
Live according to what you have learned and accepted,
what you have heard me say and seen me do.
Then will the God of peace be with you.

(Philippians 4:4-9)